After being punished, sixteen-year-old Jane became angry with her father. She stifled an urge to punch him, but awoke the next morning with a paralyzed right hand—a victim of a psychosomatic illness. Young Julio couldn't keep a job because he suffered from mood swings. When he felt "low," he wouldn't leave the house; when he felt "high," he couldn't concentrate and was belligerent. What he didn't realize was that a *chemical imbalance* had caused him to suffer from manic-depressive illness. These are just two of the interesting case reports discussed in *Don't Blame the Devil*. Here Dr. O. Quentin Hyder reveals the causes of and cures for emotional problems that are common to the Christian experience. You'll gain hope and peace of mind, as well as valuable knowledge, as you observe how problem areas can be alleviated through medical treatment. Most importantly, Dr. Hyder points the way to Jesus Christ's healing abilities which triumph over emotional difficulties.

By O. Quentin Hyder:
The Christian's Handbook of Psychiatry
The People You Live With
Shape Up
Don't Blame the Devil

O. QUENTIN HYDER

Don't Blame the Devil

Power
Books

Fleming H. Revell Company
Old Tappan, New Jersey

Scripture quotations are based on the King James Version of the Bible.

Library of Congress Cataloging in Publication Data

Hyder, O. Quentin, 1930–
   Don't blame the Devil.

   "Power Books."
   1. Pastoral psychology—Case studies. 2. Christian
life—1960–   . 3. Hyder, O. Quentin, 1930–
I. title.
BV4012.H9 1984   253.5   83-13864
ISBN 0-8007-5132-9

TO
my loved ones:
my parents and sister,
my wife,
my three children

Contents

Acknowledgments

In the almost thirty-five years I have been a Christian and in the medical profession, many persons have aided me spiritually and professionally. To them I owe a deep debt of gratitude. I am who I am largely because of their influence and inspiration.

Most special are my parents and sister, Valerie. My father, Dr. Roland I. Hyder (1903–1975), beloved family doctor, encouraged me to become a physician and helped support me through medical school. My mother, Dr. Louise Hobbs, also a physician, now retired, has inspired me more than anyone else both to be compassionate to others, and always to remain a student. Almost eighty years old, she is still taking college courses for credit and provides living proof that a sharp mind contributes to a healthy body.

My spiritual conversion and early Christian growth were predominantly brought about through the influence of Arthur H. Lewis, my tutor at prep school; the preaching, at Cambridge University, of the Reverend E. J. H. Nash and Dr. Donald Grey Barnhouse, of Philadelphia; and the Bible teaching, in London, of evangelist Tom Rees, the Reverend John R. W. Stott, and Dr. D. Martyn Lloyd-Jones. I also acknowledge the influence of devout men of God in assemblies of Plymouth Brethren, both in England and America.

The outstanding Bible teacher Reverend Everett L. Fullam, rector of Saint Paul's Episcopal Church, in Darien, Connecticut, presently encourages me in continuing spiritual growth and in the pursuit of a Master of Divinity degree at New York Theological Seminary.

I especially appreciate the professional help of Lawrence C. Kolb, M.D., former chairman of the department of psychiatry, College of Physicians and Surgeons, Columbia University, where I did my psychiatric training. Robert April,

M.D., associate professor of neurology at New York Medical College, has also been invaluable in helping me pass the American Board examination in psychiatry and neurology.

I owe a great deal to my professional associate and friend L. Charles Carr, Ph.D., and to our administrative assistant, Mrs. Gloria Shaw, with whom we pray regularly in our Christian counseling center. Mrs. Shaw has frequently played a significant part in giving comfort and advice to many of our patients and clients.

To my patients, from whom I have learned so much, I owe a great debt. Through their dialogues with me I have been increasingly instructed and matured and have become better prepared to help others.

My thanks also go to Mrs. Elizabeth Brooks, who always makes herself available for extra secretarial work, and to Mrs. Dayna Kaye, a good friend from the Ridgeway Alliance Church, in White Plains, New York, who not only typed almost the entire manuscript, but also studied it thoroughly and made many suggestions and changes that invariably improved the finished product.

Finally I acknowledge my indebtedness to my beautiful wife, Lou Ann, who has created the loving home of warmth and security in which we are raising our three healthy and happy children: Jennifer, Justyn, and Julie.

Preface
A Letter From the Author

Dear Christian Reader:

A quick glance at *Don't Blame the Devil* will tell you that
this book briefly covers many topics. I have purposely designed it to include many common, painful emotional and
spiritual problems that I have met in nearly twenty years of
psychiatric practice.

For new Christians, I offer this book as an aid to spiritual
growth. They will easily relate to several areas considered
here. Achieving spiritual maturity requires an awareness of
problems in the Christian life and a continual growth in the
processes that are part of attaining this goal. Much humility,
moral strength, and often supernatural power are required
to take responsibility for our own actions, to be able to say,
"I am wrong. It is my fault. I am responsible." The key to
this book is the need for Christians to take responsibility for
their own lives and to balance this with a right view of the
sovereignty of God in the affairs of man.

In my practice I see many troubled persons, mainly
Christians who are living defeated lives; they have failed to
understand the nature and causes of their problems or have
not dealt with them correctly and responsibly. When self-
esteem was threatened, they defended themselves by dis-
claiming responsibility for failure. When in trouble, Christians tend to blame God, other persons, or the devil. This
book could just as appropriately have been entitled *Don't
Blame God* or *Don't Blame Your Parents.*

Don't Blame the Devil is not a book of theory. It is a practical account of real-life problems and some of their answers
in the lives of those I have counseled.

I have dealt with each topic more or less distinctly, and

the chapters may be read in any order. I recommend that you first read the ones most relevant to you or someone you know.

After each chapter are questions for private contemplation or group discussion; this will stimulate further thought on the main issues. I have also included suggestions for further reading. These are designed to help you pursue in more depth the solutions to problems faced by you or a loved one.

I pray that the God of love whom we worship will use some of these pages to help you and your loved ones find greater health, joy, and spiritual maturity in the few remaining years in space and time that He may graciously grant us.

Your brother in Christ's service,
O. QUENTIN HYDER

"Guilty, with an explanation, Your Honor."

Drawing by Lorenz; ©1982
The New Yorker Magazine, Inc.

1

Christianity and Psychiatry
Medical, Emotional, and Spiritual Problems

I was alone, very alone, piloting a tiny, single-engine airplane over London when I became trapped in some low clouds. Suddenly I could no longer see the ground and was unable to tell if I was flying straight and level or going out of control.

In front of me were the essential instruments: the turn-and-bank indicator, the artificial horizon, the climb-and-descent indicator, two others that showed my airspeed and altitude, and a directional compass. With uninterrupted, intense concentration on these, I was for a short while able to keep the plane on an even keel.

Within a few minutes, however, my concentration lapsed, and I began to rely on my own sense of attitude from the balance mechanisms in my inner ears, but these only work in conjunction with a firm basis for sight or touch, which I lacked. I could see only cloud all around me and could touch only the stick and rudder pedals, since I was tightly strapped in.

Suddenly I realized that the nose of the plane was pointing steeply up; my airspeed quickly dropped; and the plane stalled and started to go into a spin toward the ground.

15

"Lord, save me," I muttered, half terrified of being killed, and half mad at myself for my stupidity.

The spin quickly took me below the cloud base, and the instant I saw the ground I was immediately able to restore level flight. Mercifully I still had a few hundred feet to spare. I thanked God that there were no high hills in the area and that I was safe. I remembered His promise in Deuteronomy 33:27: "The eternal God is thy refuge, and underneath are the everlasting arms. . . ."

This incident has become an analogy, for me, of the Christian life, in which we need to keep our attention on the facts that form the foundation of our faith. As long as I relied objectively on the instruments, I could keep the airplane on course. Once I started relying on my own subjective feelings, I was headed for destruction.

So, too, with the Christian experience. If we keep our minds and hearts focused on the historic facts of divine inspiration of Scripture, the incarnation and resurrection of Christ, on God's eternal sovereignty, and His mercy, provision, and love toward us, we will experience victorious lives. But once we live on the basis of our feelings, we quickly veer off course. Faith based on feelings is like a plane without a pilot.

The Christian faith is not a purely emotional experience, though emotions are a part of it. Our faith is based on history and the objective reality that ". . . God was in Christ, reconciling the world unto himself . . ." (2 Corinthians 5:19). If we look at the problems in the world around us as I looked at the clouds, it could lead to disaster or defeat. For victory we need to be constantly "Looking unto Jesus the author and finisher of our faith . . ." (Hebrews 12:2).

I am a Christian, a physician, and a psychiatrist, and each day I see many people who have wandered off course with a wide range of problems. These vary from psychosis to marital communication breakdowns, from obsessive thoughts to obesity, and from anxiety to guilt.

Most of my patients are true believing Christians of many sorts: fundamentalists, evangelicals, charismatics, devout Catholics, and a variety of denominational adherents with widely divergent levels of spiritual experiences or commitments. They all have in common however the need to straighten out internal personal or external relationship problems that they have been unable to deal with themselves. They need to get their lives back on course.

The causes of these problems are also various. Some problems are purely spiritual in nature, requiring of the believer a fresh understanding of the essentials of the Christian faith and a renewed willingness to make a rededication to a new commitment to Christ as Lord. Many such Christians are living like a pilot who is not relying on his instruments to guide him.

Some experience emotional or psychological problems that respond to counseling: They need to talk out their inner tensions and to make some life-changing decisions to improve their ability to cope with routine responsibilities. These people are like a pilot who wants to watch his instruments, but whose internal tensions prevent his concentration on them.

Others face social or marital problems and need to discover the basics of how to improve their interpersonal relationships, communications, and priorities. These live like a pilot who disregards the fundamental information his instruments give.

A fourth group suffers from medical problems due to biochemical imbalances in the brain, causing upsets in mood, thought processes, or behavior. These are like a pilot who has lost the use of his instruments through an electrical failure in the plane.

However, nothing in life is black and white. Almost all those whom I see have several overlapping problems, which are frequently interrelated. For example a depression of medical origin can result in a believer fearing he has lost his salvation. Anxiety can lead to uncontrollable, repetitive, un-wanted sexual or blasphemous flash thoughts. Neurotic feeling may cause physical aches and pains. Anger, resent-ment, bitterness, hostility, or jealousy can lead to ulcers, co-litis, or high blood pressure. Physical illness can result in spiritual depression, with negative thinking leading to loss of faith in God's love and care.

Some well-meaning Christians believe that any mental illness is of demonic origin and teach that the cure is purely spiritual. While not denying the devil's activity in this world, Christian healing should include the medical resources God has given us to use, in addition to prayer and biblical coun-seling.

In my practice, I see many persons who have psychologi-cal, personality, or relational difficulties, which benefit from discussion or counseling. Others have neurotic experiences caused by chemical imbalances, and these respond to medi-cal treatment. Almost all need spiritual help through in-creased fellowship, Bible study, and prayer.

Most sufferers need an integrated approach that involves the physical, psychological, and spiritual components. Total health is to be well in body, mind, and spirit. If any one part is sick, the whole person is incomplete. It is my goal to effect total healing.

God is the ultimate healer, ". . . for I am the Lord that healeth thee" (Exodus 15:26). Sir William Osler said, "I treat: God heals." I also do all I can to bring healing to my patients, through sharing relevant Bible passages, counsel-ing, listening, and when necessary, through the prescription of specific medications. I also use and rely on prayer. I pray *for* all my patients daily, and whenever they are willing, I pray *with* them as well, usually at the end of our sessions to-gether.

God heals, but He usually chooses to use human means. All physicians need to be humble enough to recognize that God sometimes chooses to step in and produce miraculous cures they cannot account for. More often God seems to take time producing the healing by means of the spiritual, psychological, and medical treatments He has made available.

It is my hope that this book will help healing come to pass in your life or in the life of a loved one.

Questions

1. Think and pray about the verses quoted in this chapter: 2 Corinthians 5:19; Hebrews 12:2; Exodus 15:26; Deuteronomy 33:27. How could they apply to you personally?

2. Have you had any problems with your feelings adversely affecting your faith? Share examples from your own Christian experience.

3. What are your views on mind-altering drugs? Do you think they should be used if prescribed by a physician or avoided even if one recommends them? What are your reasons?

4. Is your Christian life off course? What could or should you do to get it back on course again? As a group discuss your off-course problems and their remedies.

5. Discuss in your group views on the personal Christian faith as it relates to psychological or emotional problems. What kinds of feeling or thinking disorders are essentially spiritual problems? What other kinds are medical problems? In what different ways should these problems be treated?

For Further Study

Allen, Charles L. *God's Psychiatry.* Old Tappan, N.J.: Fleming H. Revell, 1953.

Collins, Gary R. *Search for Reality: Psychology and the Christian.* Santa Ana, Calif.: Vision House, 1969.

Nee, Watchman. *The Normal Christian Life.* Fort Washington, Pa.: Christian Literature Crusade, 1957.

Wittman, E. C., and Bollman, C. R. *Bible Therapy.* New York: Simon & Schuster, 1979.

2

"The Devil Made Me Do It"

God's Sovereignty and Man's Responsibility

Dick was a seminary student intent on preparing himself to become a pastor. All had gone well through college, where he had obtained excellent grades and had fallen in love with the girl of his dreams. Unhappily, she had jilted him in his second seminary year, and he became so despondent that one Friday night he impulsively took an overdose of sleeping pills. Mercifully, his roommate, Chris, had had a change in his plans for the weekend and returned unexpectedly to find Dick in a coma. Chris called for an ambulance, and Dick had his stomach washed out in a local hospital emergency room and was hospitalized for a few days. After discharge his parents arranged for him to see me for follow-up treatment.

"The devil made me do it," Dick began. "I just felt out of control, as if some evil force had taken over in my spirit. It frightens me to think that if Chris had not come back, I might be dead by now."

"Any chance of your trying it again?" I asked.

"I don't think so. I sure hope not. I think I've accepted Kay finding another boyfriend and I'm trying to trust God for my future career and marriage with another woman. But there's no hurry for that. I want to be ordained first."

"What's all this about an evil force?" I questioned. "And what does that have to do with your personal spiritual life?"

"Hmm, come to think about it," Dick said, "I suppose I have been somewhat confused recently about God's purpose for my life and about what I ought to be doing with it. I sometimes feel like a pawn in a chess game going on between God and the devil, and I'm being manipulated by both sides. I guess that's what I mean about an evil force."

"Where are you at spiritually?"

"Well I was saved in my prep-school years through a summer camp I attended. There I heard the Gospel clearly preached and first understood the need for a personal commitment to Christ. When I was a sophomore in college, I felt God's leading into the ministry. My church has been so spiritually dead for so long I really felt God had called me to work with the renewal and revival that was going on within it."

"Has any of that changed?" I inquired.

"I guess not," Dick responded, "at least now, today, I feel a fresh sense of calling. But last month I was really down and uncertain. In retrospect I can see that I had wrongly assumed that God had given me Kay as a future wife, and when she left me, it was as if my whole world collapsed."

"What's your belief about the sovereignty of God in your life?" I asked him.

"If you'd asked me that a month ago," Dick said, "I'd probably have been pretty vague, but God certainly was sovereign that Friday night. If I ever needed proof, I got it then. You know I really wanted to die that day. I didn't just take two or three pills. I took the whole bottle. Thank God Chris returned when he did. I wasn't expecting him until Sunday evening."

"Yes, your parents told me it had been a serious attempt," I said. "That's why they want me to go over a few matters of your personal philosophy with you, to help you to re-evaluate your sense of direction in life."

"Typical," Dick interrupted. "Sounds just like them. They're not saved and can't understand my wanting to become a pastor. They wanted me to go to business school and make a lot of money."

"Don't knock them, Dick. They love you and have been giving you a first-class education. They're even supporting you in seminary, in spite of their not appreciating your motivation. Now they're paying me to help you. They're not expecting me to persuade you to go to business school. They're actually proud that you've taken an unusual route in life. They *do* see the pastoral ministry as a high calling, and they respect you for your choice."

"Yeah, I'm sorry," Dick agreed. "They're really good folks, I guess." He paused for a few seconds while his train of thought changed, and I didn't interrupt him. Suddenly he said, "So what's all this about you straightening out my thinking?"

"That's putting it a bit strongly," I replied. "You know that only God can do that. I just want to help you to think through the matter of the balance between God's sovereignty and your responsibility in your life."

"Oh, the divine paradox," Dick quipped. "Sounds like predestination and free will again."

"Well, it's not actually a paradox," I said. "It's what you theologians call an *antinomy*."

"Never thought of myself as a theologian," he said, "but I suppose some people think that's what seminary is all about. In any case what's the difference between a *paradox* and an *antinomy?* I've heard the word, but I'm not sure what it means."

"A paradox is not a real incompatibility," I began. "It is just a figure of speech or a play on words. For example we learn in church that 'service is perfect freedom.' Paul said, 'As sorrowful, yet always rejoicing; as poor, yet making many rich; as having nothing, and yet possessing all things' [2 Corinthians 6:10]. He also said, '. . . when I am weak, then am I strong,' [2 Corinthians 12:10].

"Those statements are apparently incompatible to the person who has no spiritual understanding. But you and I know what they mean. We could have learned that commitment to God's service gives one a greater freedom from sin. Paul meant that, in spite of distressing circumstances, he was at all times able to rejoice in the Lord, knowing that God was in control of those circumstances. He also meant that, though he had little money, with God's help he could enrich others spiritually and that, when he felt the most helpless, God gave him the faith to believe that His divine strength was undergirding him.

"So a paradox is a purely verbal structure, comprehensible to those with insight, but used as a powerful way of making a point. An antinomy on the other hand is not comprehensible. It is an apparent incompatibility between two seemingly opposite truths."

"Like predestination and free will?" Dick asked.

"Yes," I affirmed, "but also God's sovereignty and man's responsibility, which is the issue relevant to your present situation."

"Go on," Dick encouraged, looking very interested. "Tell me more."

"Well, an antinomy is not just found in philosophy or theology," I went on. "For example in physics evidence shows that light consists of particles, but also travels in waves. Physicists have tried so far without success to integrate these two different concepts for which there are equally valid evidences: So they've had to accept both theories and deal with their frustration in being unable to rule out one in favor of the other or to reconcile them in any way.

"It's the same with God's sovereignty and our responsibility," I went on. "Both doctrines are very clearly taught in the Scriptures.

"First, the Bible teaches that God both orders and controls all things, including all human actions, in accordance with His eternal purpose. For example, when Joseph revealed himself to his brothers, he said, '. . . it was not you that sent me hither, but God . . . ,' and, '. . . ye thought evil against me; but God meant it unto good . . .' [Genesis 45:8, 50:20]. David stated, 'The steps of a good man are ordered by the Lord . . .' [Psalms 37:23]. Solomon declared, 'A man's heart deviseth his way: but the Lord directeth his steps," and, "The king's heart is in the hand of the Lord . . . he turneth it whithersoever he will' [Proverbs 16:9; 21:1]. Paul, speaking of God the Father, said, '. . . We . . . being predestinated according to the purpose of him who worketh all things after the counsel of his own will' [Ephesians 1:11].

"Now the teachings that man is responsible for his attitudes, choices, and the things he does and that he will be rewarded or punished by God accordingly are seemingly irreconcilable with sovereignty. But to the fallen couple in Eden God said: 'I will greatly multiply thy sorrow. . . . cursed is the ground for thy sake; in sorrow shalt thou eat of it all the days of thy life' [Genesis 3:16, 17]. Solomon also wrote: 'As righteousness tendeth to life: so he that pursueth evil pursueth it to his own death' [Proverbs 11:19].

"Concerning our actions, in Matthew twenty-five Jesus tells the parable of the wise and foolish virgins, the parable of the talents, and says of acts of compassion toward one's neighbor, '. . . Inasmuch as ye have done it unto one of the least of these my brethren, ye have done it unto me' [verse 40]. To those who were not compassionate, He states, '. . . ye did it not to me. And these shall go away into everlasting punishment: but the righteous into life eternal' [verses 45, 46].

"God will judge us for what we do. Paul speaks of the '. . . revelation of the righteous judgment of God; Who will render to every man according to his deeds' [Romans 2:5, 6]. In his vision of the great white throne John wrote, 'And I saw the dead, small and great, stand before God; and the books were opened ... and the dead were judged out of those things which were written in the books, according to their works" [Revelation 20:12]."

"Kind of sobering words," Dick said. "But how does all this jibe with forgiveness and redemption?"

"Good question," I replied. "Let me apply all these truths to your particular situation."

"First of all your suicide attempt was the product of your own free will, and you were solely responsible for it. It was your choice. The devil didn't make you do it. As a Christian the Holy Spirit dwells within you, protecting you from the devil; but your free will can at all times reject God. That's what living by faith is all about: obeying, not rejecting God. Without redemption you would have been held totally accountable for your self-destructive action, had you succeeded. In this respect God is your judge.

"However, God is also your King, and in this sovereign capacity He stepped in in mercy to rescue you from the natural effects of your own foolishness. He was not going to let your sin prevent you from fulfilling His purposes for your life. You see the antinomy here: You are on the one hand a responsible moral agent; on the other hand you are also under divine control. Both are truth and reality.

"It is not so much that they are apparently incompatible—though this is indeed the case—but rather that, since both are clearly taught in Scripture, we need to accept them as facts. There is no purpose in trying to reconcile divine sovereignty and human responsibility. They are two sides of a divine mystery that our finite minds cannot comprehend. We need to accept both: to make morally right decisions and act responsibly and also to recognize that God is ultimately in control. He will not permit His purposes to be frustrated by our sin.

"Now the Bible verses that describe His punishment apply primarily to the unrepentant, at least in the eternal sense. The redeemed are saved and eternally secure, but the principles of cause and effect still apply. If we as Christians sin, we might still suffer the natural or human consequences, even though, after repentance, God has forgiven us. Usually Christians' suffering as a result of sin is the 'chastening' experience described in Hebrews twelve, in which God allows pain in order to yield the '. . . peaceable fruit of righteousness unto them which are exercised thereby' [verse 11]."

"How about the philosophy of determinism?" Dick questioned. "Are God's sovereignty and predestination a form of religious determinism?"

"No, Dick. Determinism is a pagan ethical philosophy that does not see God as intervening in the affairs of mankind. It does not recognize the control God exercises over man's actions. This theory says that everything that happens to you, including moral choices you make, is determined by previously existing causes. Your background and previous experiences influence what you are, and therefore you cannot help what you choose to do. This is completely contrary to biblical teachings.

"The Bible says that you have free will and are responsible for your moral decisions, but it also includes the doctrine of His sovereignty—and this includes predestination—which tells you that God exercises overall restraint on what you decide and how you act."

"What else should I know about all this?" Dick asked.

"Okay, let's consider various life experiences and try to see how responsibility and sovereignty apply either to you personally or to others whom you will be counseling in your future ministry.

"First with life itself: We have already agreed God intervened to rescue you so that you might serve him for a lifetime. But during your lifetime, from now on, you remain responsible to keep your body healthy and your mind alert, while trusting God to keep you safe and able to continue in His service. In practical terms this means, for example, driving safely, eating moderately, exercising regularly, and avoiding situations that you know to be potentially danger-ous. These are *your* responsibility.

"*God* is responsible for your life span and your state of health, if you fulfill your side of the deal. He will not take you to be with Himself one second before or after the time He has ordained for you. Job said, 'Though he slay me, yet will I trust in him. . . .' [Job 13:15]. If you can believe this, you can go through life in peace, trusting God that nothing, even death, can happen to you outside His divine purposes."

"I do believe that," Dick said, "and it is a great source of comfort to me."

"Good," I went on. "I'm glad your faith is so well founded. Next let's consider healing, again both for yourself and for others. God in His sovereign mercy is the ultimate healer. He made our bodies and minds with the innate abil-ity to heal. Right now He is in the process of healing you of the depression you experienced when Kay left you. He also provided medical help to heal you or prevent you from suf-fering from the full effects of your overdose.

"In the future, when sick, your responsibility is to seek the appropriate medical help that God has provided. Think of medical know-how, although somewhat limited, not as man's wisdom, but as God's gift to us, which He intends us to use. So don't take any more overdoses, and if you get sick, get yourself a physician; but trust the Great Physician to ef-fect the healing."

"Well, I'm in pretty good health right now," Dick said, "but I'll bear that in mind for myself in later years or in counseling others, and no, I won't take any more overdoses! But now what about my other physical and emotional needs? What about a wife?"

"I have no doubt, Dick, that if God has called you to be a pastor, He will soon bring a wife into your life. You will need a wife in a job like that, unless you are especially called to be celibate, which is very rare. Solomon said, 'Whoso findeth a wife findeth a good thing, and obtaineth favour of the Lord' [Proverbs 18:22].

"Your responsibility in this regard is to date Christian girls, avoid premarital fornication, and be patient in waiting for God's best. God's responsibility is to bring you together with the wife of His choice for you, and you for her, to give you both a lifelong love for each other and the knowledge of His timing for your union."

"Sounds very cut and dried," Dick smiled. "It can't be that simple."

"I didn't want to imply that it will be simple," I responded, "but if you live by faith, wanting only God's choice and not our own, He obligates Himself to give you the best at the right time. You and she ultimately, of course, will have to make the human decision, but if you both desire His will, God will give you the absolute certainty that you are doing the right thing."

"Any other points?" Dick said.

"Well finally," I replied, "with regard to your future ministry, that is also an area wherein you have responsibilities, but where God is also sovereign.

"In living the Christian life and growing and maturing in Christ, your responsibility is to study the Scriptures and pray daily. With regard to your preaching, personal witness, public evangelism, or private counseling, you need to prepare yourself to be an effective pastor. The Word must be proclaimed by us, His disciples, but God produces the results.

"God's responsibility is to give you the wisdom, the love, and the power of the Holy Spirit to enable you to do the task to which He has called you. You can be sure He will watch over you as He has already done and will provide for all your needs personally and for your professional ministry. He will also give you satisfaction and fulfillment in all areas of your life as you continue to serve Him."

Dick, shortly after I last saw him, graduated from semi-

nary and was ordained. He was called to a church in the
Midwest. I received a Christmas card from him recently in
which he said that all was well in his calling and that he had
just gotten engaged. I continue to pray for him that God will
go on watching over him and give him all the blessings he
needs to live a full and happy life both professionally and
personally.

Questions

1. Have you experienced the devil influencing your life?
Are you sure it was the devil? If so, what did you do about
it? If not, what else could have caused the problem? Share
your experiences with others.

2. Can a Christian be demon possessed, oppressed, or obsessed? Defend your opinions with Scripture and discuss
them with others. Should the devil be blamed for a suicide?

3. Discuss the scriptural support for both sides of the two
antinomies of predestination and free will and God's sovereignty and man's responsibility.

4. Consider some real-life examples of the four paradoxes
quoted in 2 Corinthians 6:10 and 12:10. What experiences
have you had personally with these?

5. Think and pray about verses quoted in this chapter as
they have already, or might in the future, apply to you personally: Genesis 45:8, 50:20; Psalms 37:23; Proverbs 11:19,
16:9, 21:1; Matthew 25:40, 45, 46; Romans 2:5, 6; Ephesians
1:11; Revelation 20:12.

For Further Study

Collins, Gary. *How to Be a People Helper.* Santa Ana, Calif.:
    Vision House, 1976.

Lewis, C. S. *A Grief Observed.* New York: Bantam, 1961.

Morison, Frank. *Who Moved the Stone?* Downers Grove, Ill.: Inter Varsity Press, 1930.

Packer, James I. *Evangelism and the Sovereignty of God.* Downers Grove, Ill.: Inter Varsity Press, 1961.

Tournier, Paul. *The Whole Person in a Broken World.* New York: Harper & Row, 1981.

Wise, Robert L. *When There Is No Miracle.* Ventura, Calif.: Regal, 1978.

3

"Why Doesn't God Heal Me?"

Healing: Medical and Supernatural

She was angry, hostile, and depressed. Angry at God, hostile toward me, and deeply depressed within herself. "I've been seeing you every week for two months now, and I'm feeling worse, not better."

Lynn then burst into tears and grabbed at the box of tissues on the low glass table beside her. "I'm feeling terrible. Your stupid pills aren't working. All you do is sit and listen. You haven't done anything to help me.

"Fred, my Bible-class leader, teaches that Christians shouldn't have emotional problems. He says I must have some unrepented sin in my life. I've prayed all I know how. It doesn't do any good. Why doesn't God help me? Heal me?"

She went on like this for several minutes, without allowing any interruption. During this explosive period, she was quite right. All I could do was sit and listen, knowing that her outburst was relieving a lot of pent-up tension.

Suddenly she stopped and was silent for a few seconds as she dried her eyes and cheeks. Slowly she developed a sheepish smile and glanced away.

"I'm sorry," she mumbled. "Shouldn't yell at a doctor like that. Specially didn't mean to yell at you."

"That's okay, Lynn. It's important that you said what you did. You need to ventilate your feelings, and I need to know what's going on inside you. Don't feel bad about shouting at me. It's good for our relationship that you can feel you can do it without fear of my getting upset or rejecting you."

She composed herself quickly and reached into her handbag for a piece of paper on which she had jotted a few notes about the events of the previous week.

"How do you feel now?" I asked.

"Much better, I guess. Thank you for listening, for caring." She paused for a second and then added, "Sometimes I wish I could see you every day, but I know you want me to learn to cope without you."

We then began to discuss some of the events of the past few days and how she had handled them. As I expected, some of her coping habits had not changed, but a few differences showed that she was, in fact, slowly learning to improve her attitudes and relationships. I pointed these out to her and encouraged her in her progress.

She also admitted that, even though her medications had failed to restore her in a week or two to total health, which had been her initial unrealistic expectation, they had nevertheless somewhat calmed her anxious mind, elevated her depressed mood, and conquered her insomnia.

"Fred says I should flush all my pills down the toilet, that God can heal me without them; but I guess I'm scared to do that. He also says it's bad stewardship of my money to be spending it on a 'shrink.' He says I lack faith—that I don't trust in the Lord the way I should. He says I should pray more, read the Bible more, and get as much Christian fellowship as I can every week."

"Now, Lynn, hold it a second," I interrupted. "I'm not a psychoanalyst. I don't just sit and listen, or go to sleep for that matter, while I let you ramble on. It's good for you to let out all the things that are bothering you. Talking them out really does help you to feel less depressed and less anxious.

"We need to deal with some of your problems and try to come up with some answers, but we need to take one topic at a time. I know you've got a lot on your mind, a lot you feel you have to spill out; and you *will* be able to do it all eventually, though we will need to take several sessions. What today do you think is either the most important or the most urgent problem you'd like to discuss?"

Lynn thought for a second or so and then responded, "Well, I guess the most urgent is the matter of the medications; and the most important I suppose is the main reason I'm here, to have you get me to feel and function better."

"Okay," I said. "Let's talk about the medications first. You've just said they have helped you a little bit. Well, if you stick with them, they'll continue to make you feel better. You've only been taking them a couple of weeks. They might take a month or more to reach their maximum effectiveness. Any side effects?"

"Yeah, they give me a dry mouth, and I feel a bit sleepy, especially in the afternoons, but I guess I can put up with them if they really start to work. By the way, how *do* they work?"

Here is a brief summary of what I told her, based on present-day knowledge and theories.

Anxiety and depression like Lynn's, and like other people's more serious disorders, are caused by chemical imbalances in the brain, which is made up of billions of long, thin, interconnecting nerve cells. These imbalances cause the impulses that are sent from one cell to the next to be disturbed. Impulses act rather like electric currents flowing down a wire, but when they reach the end of one cell, there is *not* direct contact with the beginning of the next cell, like two electric wires that are twisted together.

Transmission of the impulses takes place at a junction called a synapse, which looks rather like this:

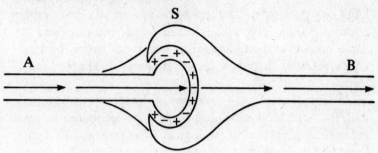

The synapse is actually a tiny sac of fluid that contains salt molecules, hormones, and a variety of other chemicals in minute quantities.

When the impulse traveling down nerve cell A reaches S, the synapse, a series of complicated changes take place in the contents of the fluid; these initiate an impulse in nerve cell B. An individual synapse is minute in size, but at any moment, this process happens to millions of them.

In a patient with a thought or emotional disorder, these synaptic transmissions are disrupted. This causes the symptoms the sufferer complains about. Neurotic and emotional disorders, such as anxiety and depression, and disorders of thinking, such as psychotic conditions like schizophrenia, paranoia, and manic-depressive illness, result from this.

Of course the precise form of the chemical imbalance determines which disorder the person experiences. Some examples give a simple idea of how this is thought to work: Too much adrenaline, a hormone produced by the adrenal glands, near the kidneys, could cause anxiety; too little might cause depression. One form of imbalance in the salt atoms could also cause depression, but another could produce mania, which is an ecstatic, irrational, high mood. An imbalance of the substance dopamine can cause a psychosis (*see* chapter five).

Other abnormal chemicals cause schizophrenia or paranoia, as evidenced by the psychotic symptoms produced in otherwise normal people who take hallucinogenic drugs like

LSD or angel dust. (Don't forget, by the way, that other popular poisons like alcohol, marijuana, nicotine, and in some people, even refined white sugar can cause thinking and emotional disorders. More on these in chapter fourteen.)

You can see that most disorders of thought or feeling, and therefore of functioning, can usually be attributed to real microanatomical and physiological abnormalities. This puts them, for the most part, into the category of medical, as opposed to spiritual, problems. Medications developed over the past thirty years can reverse the abnormal effects of these chemical imbalances. They do not always *cure* the illnesses, but they do usually help the patient to feel and function better.

Having explained all this to Lynn, I asked how she now felt about taking medications and about Fred's opinions.

"Well," she responded, "you did say that it's all theory and not really yet proven, or at least not yet fully understood: But I admit that it's beginning to make sense. I'll give the pills a try for a while longer—uh—how much longer?"

She was a lot more cheerful and hopeful by now. I encouraged her: "Stick with the present dose level, at least until I see you next week, and then we can perhaps begin to reduce it if all goes well. As you progress and improve we'll start cutting down the dose gradually.

"Eventually, of course, we want to get you to the point where you won't need them anymore, but don't cut them off suddenly by impulsively deciding to throw them all away. If you do that, you might relapse, that is, have another serious setback or breakdown. You'll find eventually—in a few weeks or a few months at most—your symptoms will improve; you'll feel normal again; and you won't need any more pills, or even me!"

"Okay, but what about Fred? What do I say to him at our next Bible study?" she questioned.

"All right." I said. "Here's what I think should be your approach.

"First of all, as Christians, we should all be in a position of humility—that is, you and Fred and I—in recognizing that God is sovereign in ruling the smallest details of our lives, because He truly loves and cares for us more even than we do for ourselves.

"God does not will executively that any of His children must suffer, but He does *permit* suffering for a purpose, which in His love and mercy, He often chooses to reveal to us later, either in this life or eternity.

"Fred is correct that God is the ultimate healer. He made our physical bodies and minds with built-in capacities to combat illness. If this were not true, we as a race, would never have survived. Fred is also right in encouraging you to enjoy more fellowship, Bible study, and prayer. However, see if you can share this concept with him.

"God has given to us two revelations: special and natural. Special revelation is the Bible, telling preeminently of God's Word, or Logos, God incarnate, Jesus Christ, our Lord and Savior.

"He also gave us an ever-increasing knowledge of nature, the creation, the whole cosmos. All the discoveries of science, including those in medicine, are part of this natural revelation. We could not have made all the many discoveries in medicine, surgery, or psychiatry that we have in the last several years outside of God's revelatory will.

"I am a Christian first: But I am also a physician. I believe that God in His mercy, especially in our present generation, has chosen to allow us to gain a vastly new volume of knowledge in the category of natural revelation, which He not only permits, but actually wants us to use.

"This is the reason why, as a Bible-believing Christian, I have no reservations about using the knowledge of medicines and counseling principles I have gained from my professional training and experience.

"I therefore believe that God wills and permits me to prescribe proven, effective, recently discovered medications. Also I am sure that any techniques of counseling or psychotherapy that I have acquired, either through professional training or by my personal biblical studies, may in His divine purpose be used by me in my daily working life helping the suffering to find healing."

"Whew—that's quite a mouthful," said Lynn, shaking her head. "It all seemed so theoretical to me at first, but you now make it sound so practical. I'll try to pass all this on to Fred; but we can't expect him to understand or agree with it all, can we?"

"No, not right away, anyway," I agreed. "But tell him to feel free to call me if he would like to discuss any of these things further with me. Even if he doesn't, I see him as your spiritual leader and advisor and would like to work in cooperation with him in helping you to grow and progress to both human and spiritual maturity. Even if we disagree on some details of method, we can still have fellowship and pray together on your behalf as brothers in Christ.

"Lynn, let me tell you one final thing before you leave. God *wants* you well. You *will* be well, either soon or later. He can choose at any time to heal you supernaturally, miraculously. That's His prerogative.

"However, God *usually* chooses to use human *means*. This is *not* the same as human *wisdom,* but rather is divinely revealed knowledge that He has chosen to give to us to fulfill His eternal purposes.

"Medical knowledge has already virtually conquered most infectious diseases, diabetes, and many surgically curable conditions, but He also has given us medications and techniques to help *reduce* suffering in emotional disorders, even if permanent cures are not yet available. God sometimes permits these for a purpose: But He also provides relief through the balanced application of His twofold revelation, spiritual and scientific."

As she left, I prayed God would indeed heal Lynn, which He did over a period of time. As she gradually improved her symptoms troubled her less, and as her depression lifted and anxiety subsided she became a happier person, more productive at work, and more pleasant to be with socially.

Her medications were gradually reduced until she needed them no more. On her final visit, Lynn announced that she was about to get married to a young man in her Bible class and move with him to another part of the country.

Many factors aided in her healing. The temporary use of medications relieved her painful symptoms and indirectly enabled her to think through her problems more clearly. Her dialogues with me gave her the opportunity to let out her bottled-up anger and resentment and to gain a lot of insight into her personality and needs.

Lynn's own determination to get well provided her with motivation to cope with her problems. Private devotions and Christian fellowship provided a support and inspiration through her darkest hours and brought her to a new spiritual maturity.

Questions

1. Lynn said she wished she could see me every day. Is there someone in your life who has become dependent on you? If so, should your Christian attitude be to encourage the dependency or work toward separation? Any scriptural support for either position? Discuss an appropriate balance between meeting others' needs and being taken advantage of by them.

2. Do you believe that seeing a psychiatrist would be bad stewardship of the Lord's money entrusted to you? Defend your opinion from the Scriptures.

3. Since God is the ultimate healer, why does He so often apparently choose not to heal or to delay healing? Discuss your attitude toward the fact that God often seems to use human means to effect cures. In this regard do you consider psychiatric conditions to be different from medical or surgical ones? If so, in what way?

4. If you or a loved one needed psychiatric help, would you go to a highly respected, experienced, competent psychiatrist, even though he was not a believing Christian? If not, why not? Would a Christian doctor necessarily be any better for you? If so, in what way?

For Further Study

Lewis, C. S. *The Problem of Pain.* New York: Macmillan, 1962.

Reed, William S. *Healing the Whole Man.* Old Tappan, N.J.: Fleming H. Revell, 1980.

Schaeffer, Edith. *Affliction.* Old Tappan, N.J.: Fleming H. Revell, 1978.

Stapleton, Ruth C. *Experiencing Inner Healing.* Waco, Tex.: Word Books, 1977.

Swindoll, Charles R. *For Those Who Hurt.* Portland, Ore.: Multnomah, 1977.

Tournier, Paul. *A Doctor's Casebook in the Light of the Bible.* New York: Harper & Row, 1976.

Tournier, Paul. *The Healing of Persons.* Westchester, Ill.: Good News Pub., 1967.

4

"How Can I Find God's Will for My Life?"

Guidance, Obedience, and Listening and Neurotic Prayer

In my practice I see many Christians who are not mentally or emotionally ill. They do not seek psychotherapy, but pastoral counseling. Often they are referred by their own pastors. Steven was one such person.

After graduating with a masters degree in history, Steven was unemployed. "I studied history because I found it fascinating," he started, "and because I felt it was God's will for me to do two more years of graduate work. I enjoyed all my courses and ended up with a high average. But now I find I can't get a job, except maybe teaching at a high-school level. But then I'd need education courses. I don't really want to do that."

We discussed some other areas in which Steven might work, but nothing seemed to fill his needs. He and his family clearly saw that he must find a job so that he could support himself and have a place of his own. His sisters were going to college, and his parents could no longer afford to send Steven to school.

"I urgently need a secure job," he said.

"So you would consider employment that is not strictly

related to your degree?" I said. "Like in a major corporation?"

"Oh, yes," he responded. "My graduate work was only
intended to be further general education. I'd be quite happy
starting at the bottom in a large corporation. History can always be a good hobby for me."

"So what you really want is God's guidance in choosing a
career. Right?"

"Oh, I definitely want God's will for my life," Steven replied. "And I'm open to any job that's available. What are
you getting at?"

"Simply this. If you want God's will for your life, He obligates Himself to guide you, show you the way, and open up
opportunities. But if you want your own way, He has no obligation to guide you. This works in every decision a Christian makes.

"What does the Bible specifically say about guidance?
First, God *is* our guide. The Prophet Jeremiah said: 'My father, thou art the guide of my youth' [Jeremiah 3:4]. David
spoke of God's obligation when he tells us: 'I will instruct
thee and teach thee in the way which thou shalt go: I will
guide thee with mine eye' [Psalms 32:8].

"But we have a responsibility, too—one of obedience.
David promises: 'The meek will he guide in judgment: and
the meek will he teach his way' [Psalms 25:9].

"If we will obey Him, God will guide us, even in the hard
times. And His direction is lifelong. Isaiah puts it this way:
'And the Lord shall guide thee continually, and satisfy thy
soul in drought . . .' [Isaiah 58:11]. The Psalmists Asaph and
David said: 'Thou shalt guide me with thy counsel, and afterward receive me to glory,' and, 'For this God is our God
for ever and ever: he will be our guide even unto death'
[Psalms 73:24, 48:14].

"The New Testament mentions guidance, too. When Za-
charias first saw his son, John the Baptist, he prophesied that
Jesus would come 'To give light to them that sit in darkness

and . . . to guide our feet into the way of peace' [Luke 1:79]. Jesus spoke of the Holy Spirit when He said: '. . . when . . . the Spirit of truth, is come, he will guide you into all truth . . .' [John 16:13]."

"Sure, I know God has my best interests in mind," Steven agreed. "But what about my part in all this? I know I can't expect the perfect job to drop in my lap without my ever looking and putting in some effort. What do you suggest I do in practical terms?"

"Well, first we can pray." We bowed our heads and petitioned the Lord for guidance for Steve.

Then I advised Steve to do all he could in searching out a job: to look in the want ads, contact employment agencies, and keep his eyes and ears open to anything and everything God presented. I also promised to put him in touch with a friend who specialized in placing junior executives.

"You need to continue to pray and study the Bible, to get plenty of Christian fellowship, and worship God on Sundays in church. Often God will use friends, a sermon, or a worship service to guide you."

We agreed that because of his urgent financial affairs, it was unlikely that God would call Steve into full-time Christian service, but he still needed to be open to that. Steve said he had never sensed a calling to it, but he was open to that, if the call came.

When he came to see me the next week, Steve had already contacted my friend and was due to go see him in a few days.

Steve had more questions. "Any principles I can follow in obeying God's will?"

"Yes," I responded. "The Christian life is a matter of daily submission and obedience to God. He does not obligate Himself to show us the future. We must follow Him one step at a time, in faith. Once we take a step, He'll show us the next. We plan for the future in human wisdom, but God often changes our plans with some totally unexpected turn of events.

"But that's what makes the Christian life exciting and interesting. We will never be bored if we seek Him daily. He knows what's around every corner and gives us only the best as we trust Him. Even pain and suffering will bring greater blessing as we live by faith.

"We can know God's will by a sense of peace. When He reveals His will, He removes all doubt. Remember the adage 'If in doubt, don't.' Uncertainty and doubt may be implanted by God to bring us back onto the right path. If we seek His will, He will be sure we do not go astray through ignorance or misunderstanding. Then we only go astray through deliberate disobedience.

"When Israel was being invaded by pagans, Isaiah exhorted them: 'And thine ears shall hear a word behind thee, saying, This is the way, walk ye in it, when ye turn to the right hand, and when ye turn to the left' [Isaiah 30:21].

"Blessings come from obedience. God told Abraham: '... [in thee] shall all the nations of the earth be blessed; because thou hast obeyed my voice' [Genesis 22:18]. When King Saul disobeyed God and did not destroy the Amalekites, Samuel said: '... Behold, to obey is better than sacrifice, and to hearken than the fat of rams' [1 Samuel 15:22].

"Responding to the high priest's command not to preach, the apostles answered, '... We ought to obey God rather than men' [Acts 5:29]. Paul told children to obey their parents and slaves to obey their masters [*see* Ephesians 6:1, 5]. Remember that we are children of God and His servants, so we, too, ought to obey Him. Speaking of Christ, the writer to the Hebrews said, '... He became the author of eternal salvation unto all them that obey him' [Hebrews 5:9].

"All right," Steven replied. "I think I understand the principles of God's blessing and our obedience, but how does God actually speak to us?"

"God can show us His way through the various means we talked about last week and this week, but the inner conviction about making the right decision, for me, has always come through listening prayer."

"What do you mean by *listening prayer?*"

"It's the opposite of *neurotic prayer,*" I told him. "Neurotic prayer is selfish and demanding. It tries to persuade God to change things for the Christian's own benefit. It shows a lack of faith and trust that God both knows what is best and will give it to the believer in His own timing.

"Neurotic prayer is marked by repetitiveness and lack of concern for others. This type of prayer almost always results from our own anxious thoughts. It becomes a monologue that spends most of its time on selfish concerns and short-changes praise, worship, thanksgiving, repentance, and intercession.

"In contrast, the Holy Spirit guides listening prayer. In it we respond to the thoughts He puts into our minds, and God directs us to pray correctly. Praying is essentially thinking and aiming our thoughts, in the form of a silent dialogue, toward God. In listening prayer, we talk *with* God, not *at* Him.

"In this prayer, the Christian gives first place to praise, adoration, and worship of Jesus as Lord—not only chronologically, but also in the time spent in these. He confesses sins and gives thanks in all things, even the disappointments in life. Intercession plays an important part, too.

"Only when these are done is it time to pray for self. We *are* supposed to ask for ourselves. God tells us to ask and seek and knock [Matthew 7:7], although He 'knoweth what things ye have need of, before ye ask him' [Matthew 6:8]. We won't receive anything from God if we do not ask. James says: ". . . Ye have not because ye ask not' [James 4:2]. But he also warns that we need to have the right attitudes; we can't be selfish or demanding or have unpure mo-

tives; 'Ye ask, and receive not, because ye ask amiss, that ye
may consume it upon your lusts' [James 4:3].

"When we have a clear conscience and are in the center of
God's will, we have the resources of heaven at our disposal.
The God who prompts the asking also provides the answer.
That's what John meant when he wrote: 'Beloved, if our
hearts condemn us not, then have we confidence toward
God. And whatsoever we ask, we receive of him, because we
keep his commandments, and do those things that are
pleasing in his sight' [1 John 3:21, 22].

"The Gospels record Jesus' many promises about God's
answers to prayers made in His name, which means that
submission is His best will for us. God has four answers:

> 'No, because it would hurt you, and I love you too
> much.'
> 'No, at least, not yet. Maybe later.'
> 'Yes, I was just waiting for you to ask.'
> 'Yes, and here's a lot more, besides.'

"Often when we are searching for answers or guidance,
we simply need to remain open to the Spirit. We must listen
to His leading and reflect His thoughts back to God. Neurotic prayer is self-initiated; true listening prayer is God ini-
tiated."

When Steve came back the next week, he had a big smile
on his face. "Your friend gave me a lot of encouragement,"
he said. "He told me that many of the best companies like
junior executives with a good liberal education, even without technical training. He's already lined up interviews with
three major companies. Although the competition is tough,
he's certain I'll land a good job eventually."

Steven went to all three interviews in the next two weeks.
One week we discussed them and the differences in them.
He was trusting God's provision, using listening prayer.

The next week Steven had another problem. "I was rejected by the first one, but the other two accepted me. Now I've got to decide between them."

Both jobs seemed exceptional to Steve. I advised him to pray about the decision, to ask God which should be his choice. Also, I said, he should talk to others: parents, pastor, my friend, and his friends, as well as me.

One month later, when Steven returned, he had a position with one of the companies. Then he asked me to share how God had guided me. Although I don't often do that in my office, I was happy to share my pilgrimage wih him.

"As you can tell by my accent," I said, "I grew up in England, where both my parents were physicians in family practice near London. I first thought about eternity when we were bombed during World War II. No one in my family was hurt, but it was a terrifying experience.

"My parents only went to church for weddings and funerals, and I was never sent to Sunday school. As a teenager, during a vacation from school, I went to a summer camp at which I first heard the Gospel clearly presented. But I didn't understand the need for a personal decision.

"Graduating from prep school, I spent a year and a half in the army and then went to Cambridge University. Donald Grey Barnhouse, the great American preacher, came there at the beginning of my first year, to conduct a mission to the students. In May, 1950, after several months of intellectual discussions and emotional upheavals, I accepted Jesus as my Savior. I was twenty years old.

"Throughout medical school, I continued to grow spiritually. While there I felt God's call to commit my life to being a medical missionary. So after I finished my internship, I spent a year in a mission hospital on the island of Malta. Through this God tested my commitment, but His plans for me did not include that I remain a missionary.

"I toured mission stations in Africa and returned to England to study surgery. Eventually I came to America to study at Johns Hopkins Hospital. Coming here was a major step of faith. But even though I could not see it, it was God's best plan.

"In 1962 I passed through my darkest time and became very depressed. A girl whom I loved very much rejected me, and I became uncertain of my professional future. On the advice of a fine Christian surgeon, I left medicine, for a time, to go to seminary in California. There I enjoyed studying a wide variety of subjects. Discussions with godly people there led me to use the combination of my medical background and biblical beliefs by becoming a psychiatrist.

"God sealed His guidance through my acceptance for a three-year psychiatry residency program back in New York City. When I graduated in 1968, I began a private practice.

"During my residency, God brought me His perfect choice for a wife. As we got to know each other I realized how all my other dating experiences had been pale images of the real thing. I got married at thirty-seven; seventeen years and three children later, we are happier than when we first met. It gets better every year, because Jesus is the head of our home.

"God still guides me and shows me more fulfilling promises for the future. I have returned to seminary part-time and am slowly working on a masters degree. Eventually I hoped to be ordained, though I am not certain how this will be combined with my psychiatric practice.

"From my earliest years God has had His hand on the daily details of my life, because He called me to be His servant. Despite frequent failures and disobedience on my part, God has remained faithful in showing me forgiveness when He has brought me to repentance. I have seen His sovereignty, bounty and mercy."

Perhaps my testimony was longer than Steven expected, but he thanked me for sharing it. As he is willing to obey God and walk in the light He provides, I know that Steven, too, will enjoy the many benefits of God's love and faithfulness.

Questions

1. Share with a group of other believers your personal testimony of God's guidance in your life. Are you conscious of His daily leading? Do you rely on Him at all times and stay close to Him through prayer and Bible study? Examine your intimate walk with the Lord.

2. Have you disobeyed God since you became a Christian? If so, what happened? Do you desire to obey God's will for your life? If so, how can you find out His will? What are the ways or principles you should pursue in order for you to follow in obedience in the future?

3. Examine your prayer life. Is some of it neurotic as described in this chapter? Is your time spent in supplication for yourself out of proportion to time spent in praise, thanksgiving, repentance, and intercession for others? Can you listen in prayer? If so, please share with others how you do it, so that they might honor the Lord by doing it also.

4. Discuss with others and contemplate for yourself these passages on guidance quoted in this chapter: Psalms 25:9, 32:8, 48:14, 73:24; Isaiah 30:21, 58:11; Luke 1:79; John 16:13. Also consider these on obedience: Genesis 22:18; 1 Samuel 15:22; Acts 5:29; Ephesians 6:1, 5; Hebrews 5:9. Then think of these on supplication: Matthew 6:8, 7:7; James 4:2, 3; 1 John 3:21, 22.

For Further Study

Bolles, Richard N. *What Color Is Your Parachute?* Berkeley, Calif.: Ten Speed Press, 1982.

Bonhoeffer, Dietrich. *The Cost of Discipleship.* New York, Macmillan, 1963.

Farah, Charles. *From the Pinnacle of the Temple: Faith or Presumption?* Plainfield, N.J.: Bridge, 1979.

Hallesby, O. *Prayer.* Minneapolis, Minn.: Augsburg, 1975.

Jabay, Earl. *The God Players.* Grand Rapids, Mich.: Zondervan, 1969.

Meyer, F. B. *The Secret of Guidance.* Minneapolis, Minn.: Bethany House, 1978.

Mumford, Bob. *Take Another Look at Guidance.* Plainfield, N.J.: Bridge, 1971.

Murray, Andrew. *The Prayer Life.* Springdale, Pa.: Whitaker House, 1981.

Nee, Watchman. *The Spiritual Man.* Translated by Stephen Kaung. New York: Christian Fellowship, 1968.

Packer, James I. *Knowing God.* Downers Grove, Ill.: Inter Varsity, 1973.

Schaeffer, Francis A. *True Spirituality.* Wheaton, Ill.: Tyndale, 1971.

Torrey, R. A. *How to Pray.* Chicago: Moody Press, n.d.

5

"I Think I'm Going Crazy!"

Psychosis: The Only Real "Mental Illness"

I hate to use *neurotic* to describe a person, because that word has such a derogatory meaning to most people. But Lynn, in chapter three suffered from the common neuroses of anxiety and depression (for more on these, see chapters eight and ten). *Neurotic* is really a technical word to distinguish her symptoms from those of the *psychotic*, who suffers from a *psychosis*. This much more serious condition never afflicted Lynn, though she might have feared that in her worst moments.

The most common psychotic condition is caused by schizophrenia, which used to be called *dementia praecox*, meaning "premature dementia," because it most often starts in young people. Very often it is not the patient who first seeks professional help, but an anxious relative.

Mrs. Brown came to see me several months ago, obviously in great distress. "It's about my son Mark. He just doesn't seem to be going anywhere or doing anything with his life. His father and I keep trying to push him to get his act together, but he just gets angry and tells us to get off his back. I wanted him to come with me, but he refused. He says we are the ones who need a psychiatrist."

"Well," I said, "It's good that you came alone this first time anyway. Give me a summary of his history and present problems. With that information, I may be able to advise you on how to cope with him or treat him if he eventually agrees to see me."

She shifted into her chair comfortably and took a deep breath. "It's a long story, but I'll give you the gist of it as briefly as I can.

"My husband and I have three children; Paul, twenty-three; Mark, twenty-one; and Jean, nineteen. We're a Christian family and all three kids have been born again. Paul has just gotten a good job, and Jean is doing very well in college. We've never had any problems with them. They are so different from Mark, especially recently.

"Mark had a very hard time finishing high school. He repeated tenth grade and never seemed to show any interest in any of his courses. He would often cut class and hang around the town. Sometimes he got together with some other truants to smoke pot or drink beer, but more often he was just off on his own. He's quite a loner. Doesn't even go out on a date."

It was already apparent to me that Mark either had a serious personality or character disorder or had been showing early signs of adolescent schizophrenia.

"He didn't want to go away to college like Paul and Jean, but we finally persuaded him to take some courses at our local community college. We should have saved our money. It was a total waste, just like high school over again. He couldn't seem to get interested in anything—except rock music. He always had his stereo on day and night, especially at night. We've had to insist that he keep the volume turned down, because he stays up until the early hours of the morning and then sleeps until noon."

"That's known as day-night reversal," I interrupted. "It's quite common in young people, but it could also be a sign of mental illness. Tell me more about how he functions and how he says he feels."

"Functions?" she questioned. "He doesn't exactly function at all. Any job he has tried to do only seems to last a very few days. He can't apply himself to anything. His attention span is very short. He does nothing. He doesn't even seem to be in touch with the real world around him. It's as if he's living completely in a fantasy world. He seems to have so many bizarre thoughts. He makes many rather peculiar comments and does some very odd things sometimes. His whole behavior is really thoroughly inappropriate."

"What do you mean by *peculiar* or *odd?*" I asked. "Can you give me some examples?"

"Well, it's impossible to have an intelligent conversation with him," she complained. "He can't seem to stick to the point in any discussion. His mind wanders continually from one irrelevant topic to another. He never seems to be able to focus on an issue. He always talks around it."

"What are his personal habits like?" I queried.

"Well, that's another problem. He doesn't take care of himself properly. He's always untidy: His clothes are a mess. He seldom brushes his teeth or takes a shower, unless my husband or I insist on it. His room always looks like a cyclone has hit it."

"And how does he relate to you and his father?"

"Hostile, as I said. Mark hates being disciplined. He complains that we do nothing but nag him. He just seems to want to be left alone. If we can even get him to join us for supper, he hardly says a word."

"How about his relationships with his brother and sister?"

"Well, when they're home at vacation or holiday times, they mainly talk with each other or us. Paul and Jean are very close; they're good kids. They try to make conversation with Mark, but soon give up because he is so unresponsive. Both complain that they seem to have nothing in common with him. I know they love him, but they just can't seem to relate to him because he is so withdrawn."

I had heard enough by now to be certain that Mark was a schizophrenic and knew from experience that without treatment he would almost certainly continue to deteriorate. It was essential that he see me or some other physician and get started in therapy.

"Mrs. Brown, does Mark know that you came to see me today?"

"Oh, yes, but I'm not sure if he thinks I came to talk about him or for my own sake."

"Okay. Now you've said that he refused your request to come to see me with you. Here's something else to try. Now that you've seen me, go home and tell Mark that you and I talked about him and about ways in which we can help him. Tell him that *I* am requesting him to see me. If he wants to come on his own, that's fine. If he wants you or his father to come with him, that's fine, too, but I would need to spend some of the time with him alone, if he's willing."

I was not surprised that Mrs. Brown called my secretary, the following week, to make an appointment for Mark. He had apparently become increasingly convinced that he needed help of some sort and was actually relieved that his mother had taken the initiative in making contact with me.

As it turned out, however, I was not to see him so soon. Over the weekend, Mr. Brown called me urgently, saying that Mark had become increasingly delusional, believing that he was being set up by organized crime to be murdered. He interpreted a TV newscast account of an underworld shooting to mean that he was to be the next victim. Matters came to a head when he accused his father and brother of cooperating with his fantasized enemies and threatened them with a large kitchen knife. They had had to call the police, who had immediately taken Mark to the emergency room of the nearest hospital. A resident psychiatrist there had promptly admitted him involuntarily on the grounds of a psychotic breakdown.

The doctor called me the following Monday to say that Mark had settled down after being started on a fairly large dose of a major (antipsychotic) tranquilizer and had signed papers for a thirty-day voluntary stay.

Christian parents and pastoral counselors need to understand the essential elements of Mark's very common type of schizophrenia, because it is a serious medical illness not normally in any way treatable solely by spiritual means such as prayer and biblical counseling. While I almost always use the Bible and prayer in my daily practice, I avoid it in dealing with a psychosis, which is just as much a medical condition as acute appendicitis, influenza, or a broken leg. As such, psychotics *first* need medical treatment to bring them back into contact with reality, *after which* psychotherapy or counseling can be beneficial.

Whereas it does not take a psychiatrist to recognise a complete mental crack-up such as Mark's, parents, pastors, and counselors should also be able to recognise the early warning signs of the schizophrenic process, so that treatment can be started early and a breakdown thereby be prevented.

Schizophrenia is a severe disorganization of the personality, affecting the intellect, the emotions, one's self-concept, and interpersonal relationships.

The *intellect* is affected by distortions in thinking in which the sufferer regresses into childlike symbolic fantasies. Thought processes become disorganized, contact with reality is lost, the rules of logic no longer hold, and bizarre ideas lead to confusion. In extreme cases the thinking distortions can lead to *delusions,* which are false convictions not changeable by reason or logic; *illusions,* which are incorrect interpretations of things seen; and *hallucinations,* which are usually internal sensations occurring without any external cause, such as hearing voices when no one is speaking.

The emotions are affected by creating the so-called split personality. The split however does not mean two different personalities, but rather the existence of a split or discrepancy between feelings and thinking. Examples are such responses as inappropriate smiling or even laughter when discussing a sad or serious topic; apathy or aloofness, with loss of enthusiasm, in matters formerly of interest; and rigidity of mood, which is a flat, unvarying emotional state unaffected by variations in external, normally stimulating, situations.

The patient's *self-concept* is affected by a loss of ability to differentiate between stimuli coming from within himself and those from the real world outside. He is confused between reality and fantasy, between his own thoughts and those of others. He is not sure where the boundary is between himself and the outside, and this seriously disturbs his sense of self-identity.

Interpersonal relationships are naturally adversely influenced by all these problems. They lead to an inability to make or keep a friendship, alienation from even intimate family members, and the loss of the capability of relating either affectionally or in conversation with others. These problems in turn lead to a chronic defect in his capacity to experience pleasure and develop fear, distrust, and feelings of rejection.

There are many different types of schizophrenia, but a discussion of their classification is not needed here. (*See* the bibliography at the end of this chapter.)

For several decades psychiatrists have tried to come up with psychological theories that could explain in cause-and-effect terms how schizophrenia develops. Nothing definite or commonly agreed has yet been produced. We can however see three definite factors which at least partially explain the illness: inheritance, stress, and biochemical imbalance.

Inheritance is almost certainly a factor as evidenced by the fact that taking a careful family history of a schizophrenic will nearly invariably produce information about other relatives having been similarly affected, usually one of a senior generation. This genetic tendency, however, seems quite random in its distribution. Mark was affected, but his siblings were spared. However, they in turn could hand down the vulnerability to their children. Mrs. Brown told me that her own father's sister had been psychiatrically hospitalized several times and had eventually committed suicide.

Stress is also thought to be necessary to produce the actual schizophrenic breakdown in someone like Mark, who was genetically predisposed to it. In his case he experienced several stressors. He had a problem in adolescence adjusting to the increased demands of his academic program; his parents put pressure on him not to become a failure, rather than encouraging him within his potential to be a success. The middle child of three often tends to be the most neglected one in any family. Never an extravert to begin with, Mark experienced increased peer rejection through his teenage years; he started drinking alcohol long before the legal drinking age (before his brain was fully matured) and partook frequently in smoking both cigarettes and marijuana (thereby further damaging his brain) in a desperate effort to conform with his peers. College and job failure still further lowered his self-esteem, and in seeing himself as a total failure, he protected himself from reality by regressing into his more safe and comfortable world of fantasy.

Biochemical imbalance, especially affecting the brain, is thought today to be the most likely actual cause of schizophrenia and of psychotic breakdowns. You will remember that in chapter three I explained that a chemical imbalance in the synaptic fluid between millions of nerve cells in the brain causes clinical neurotic and psychotic symptoms. In the case of schizophrenia, according to the *dopamine hypothesis,* the most up-to-date theory, symptoms are caused by the synaptic imbalance between the two neurotransmitters, dopamine and adrenaline, which were previously mentioned. Neurotransmitters—the chemicals in the fluid in the synapse (the sac that forms the gap between nerve endings)—send the nerve impulse from one cell to the next.

The details are of course very complicated and at best so far merely theoretical. However, strong evidence shows that the specific antipsychotic medications now used in the treatment of schizophrenia reverse the abnormal symptoms and bring a large measure of clinical recovery, if not permanent cure.

This is exactly what happened with Mark. The medications he took in the hospital quickly restored him to reality contact, and he became cooperative with his doctors and nurses. During the month he was an inpatient, his medication dosage was adjusted to his optimal level, and he was seen by a psychiatrist five or six hours a week, which enabled him to talk out many of the stresses he had experienced, especially those that had precipitated his breakdown.

After discharge, he agreed to see me, with his parents initially, and later by himself. Though no longer psychotic, he remained a chronic schizophrenic and needed to continue his medications at a reduced level to prevent further breakdowns, alleviate the recurrence of anxiety attacks, and reduce his self-destructive overreactions to stress.

The goals of psychotherapy with him were initially to reinforce the progress he had already made in the hospital, especially in the area of self-understanding and restoring a higher sense of self-worth. He also had to learn to face the reality of his emotional deficiencies and mental disabilities, but only so as to prevent future lowering of self-esteem. He was also encouraged over a period of several months to strive to rise above his limitations and regain an ever-increasing social adaptation.

He never wanted to return to college, which might well have been too much for him, but he eventually obtained a not too stressful job. When I recently saw him, he said he had joined the YMCA, had begun to make a few friends, and had even started dating a neighbor's daughter, whom he had met in his church youth group.

I still see him about every three months to renew his medication prescriptions and check up on his continuing progress. He and his parents and siblings have accepted his disabilities now and relate well to each other, providing the supportive family group that is his continuing need. He also takes his personal faith seriously and finds that both his daily devotions and his Christian fellowship remind him constantly of God's healing and sustaining hand lovingly guiding him through life.

Questions

1. Discuss how you would cope if you had someone like Mark living with you. How would you handle his hostility and anger, his belligerence and rebellion, his apathy and lack of interest, his self-centeredness, his fantasy life and loss of reality contact, his bizarre behavior, his untidiness and lack of hygiene, his poor communication, his unwillingness to get help, his loneliness, and the acute internal pain you know he must be suffering? Discuss each symptom separately.

2. Why does God permit mental illness? Is it of God, of the devil, or a natural part of human life? Is it a sin to be mentally or emotionally sick? Is it an evidence of some other sin? Is it a punishment for sin? Should treatment be primarily medical or spiritual, or both? If both, when should each be used?

3. Are you afraid of mental illness in yourself? In others? Do you have the attitude that it could never happen to you? In what ways are people with emotional or thinking disorders a threat to you personally or to society as a whole?

4. Under what circumstances would it be a compassionate Christian act to: take (or keep) a mentally-ill family member into your home? Arrange for a foster family or halfway house for him or her? Arrange for voluntary outpatient treatment? Arrange for involuntary hospitalization?

For Further Study

Frazier, Shervert H., and Carr, Arthur C. *Introduction to Psychopathology.* New York: Macmillan, 1974.

Kolb, Lawrence C. *Modern Clinical Psychiatry.* Philadelphia, Pa.: W. B. Saunders, 1982.

Minirth, Frank B. *Christian Psychiatry.* Old Tappan, N.J.: Fleming H. Revell, 1977.

Nagera, Humberto. *Early Childhood Disturbances, the Infantile Neuroses and the Adult Disturbances.* New York: International Universities, 1966.

6

"I Keep Having Horrible Thoughts"

Uncontrollable Thoughts, Phobias, and Paranoia

Many Christians have come to see me, complaining of uncontrollable thoughts. These thoughts take many forms, cover a wide variety of topics, are always distressing to the sufferer, and have in common with one another that they are recurrent, repetitive, seemingly unavoidable, and continually disruptive to daily functioning. They are usually a symptom of underlying anxiety.

The technical adjective applied to these thoughts is *obsessive-compulsive*. An *obsession* is a recurrent thought that uncontrollably pops into the conscious mind. A *compulsion* is a recurrent action, usually one done frequently, used as a means of avoiding extreme anxiety. They are often related, because obsessive thoughts are frequently associated with compulsive, equally uncontrollable, ritualistic actions. These actions seem to reduce the anxiety of the individual, but can drive the people lived with or worked with absolutely up the wall with impatience, frustration, and even reactive anger!

Mary is a thirty-two-year-old mother of four who had been raised in a very strict home. Her parents had through-

61

out her growing years put constant pressure on her and her siblings to be tidy, clean, organized, and prompt. Although she couldn't remember it, I found out from her mother that Mary had been the most difficult of her children to toilet train. As early as the age of two, her mother reported that Mary had developed a power struggle between herself and her parents, and as she grew older she became a more and more rebellious child and teenager.

She would frequently alternate between submissiveness and defiance. Sometimes, through fear or guilt, she made efforts to conform with parental demands. At other times she would fly into a rage and become obstinate, rude, disobedient, or negligent. The result was unpredictable, inconsistent attitudes and behavior.

However, as she matured Mary's strong will produced some positive traits. Soon after starting in college, she realized she was no longer in school to please her parents or teachers, but was there for her own benefit. The pressures imposed upon her as a child and adolescent she now imposed upon herself. She completely switched, in just a short span of time, from being rebellious to being success oriented.

Up to a point these changes were good. Mary became very orderly, serious, hardworking, reliable, conscientious, disciplined, and able to persevere with difficult academic studies. She got excellent grades in school, not so much because she was bright, but because of her obsession to achieve distinction.

Unfortunately she also developed some negative traits. Mary's attitudes led to introverted behavior, which resulted in her having few friends and little fun through college. She became perfectionistic, inflexible, and rigid in her behavior and relationships. Nevertheless her physical attractiveness led soon after college to a reactivation of a relationship with a former high school sweetheart, resulting in marriage in her early twenties.

Things went well in the early days of her marriage, but ten years and four children later, she started experiencing the obsessive thoughts that led to her coming to see me.

"I keep having horrible thoughts," she complained. "They keep coming back into my mind again and again, and I can't get rid of them. They are absurd, and they're making me depressed."

"What are they about?" I questioned.

"I'm ashamed to tell you," she confessed. "They're sometimes of violence, but more often they're either sexual or blasphemous—or worst of all, both. God knows I don't really mean them, but they're really disturbing my religious life. I'd be mortified if my priest found out, so I've quit going to confession or mass."

It took about three sessions for her to come to the point of describing her obsessive thoughts in detail, but after she had shared them with me, she reported that though she still had them, they bothered her less. Also, a brief course of an antidepressant medication helped reduce their frequency and severity.

I reassured her that her problem was a psychological and not a spiritual one. Her spontaneous flash thoughts were 95 percent not her responsibility, and as such she should not see herself as blameworthy. I told her that they represented a resurrection of material from years back that was repressed in her unconscious mind and had suddenly started popping back into awareness. She couldn't help these happening and therefore shouldn't feel guilty or ashamed.

I also taught her about the practice of suppression. As soon as she became aware of the recurrent thought, she should immediately and deliberately think of something else, preferably something pleasurable that she could dwell on for several seconds. While concentrating on this alternative thought, the unwanted one gradually returns to the unconscious.

In the context of positive thinking, I reminded her of

Paul's admonition to the Philippians: "Finally, brethren, whatsoever things are true, honest, just, pure, lovely, or of good report; if there be any virtue and if any praise, think on these things" (*see* Philippians 4:8).

She was to continue thinking about the pleasure until the bad thought went away, which usually takes less than a minute. I assured her that with practice she would soon get to the point where it would both recur less frequently and also trouble her less.

Talking through her strict upbringing and her later self-imposed, controlled characteristics helped her to understand the origin of her problem. Once she understood that her thoughts were a form of displaced anxiety, things improved rapidly. She had nothing to be anxious about. Her marriage was secure, her children all healthy, and she was living a full and satisfying life as a housewife, mother, and a contributing member of her local community.

I saw two compulsive young men last year with similar conditions. Bill is a teenager who developed the obsessive thought that germs from the air kept falling on his hands. This made him very anxious, until he went to the bathroom to wash them. Over a period of a few weeks, the need to do this became so frequent that at one point he was unable to stay in his classroom, and he had to take a short medical leave of absence from his school.

Charlie was a young, new employee working in a major multinational company. He developed a condition known as *folie du doute* (French for "foolishness of doubt"), manifesting indecision, vacillation, persistent doubting, and obsessive ruminations leading to repeated acts aimed at dispelling his irrational concerns. Before leaving work, he would have to check several times that his desk was locked. Even after leaving the building, he would become anxious again and return to his office to check his desk again, frequently missing his train home. Much of his paperwork had to be checked and rechecked by him, which significantly slowed his productivity and made his boss very angry, leading to threats that he would be fired.

At home before going to bed he would have to check and recheck that every door and window in his house was locked. This and his severe, persistent inability to make decisions upset his wife so much that she once threatened to leave him.

Like many, both Bill and Charlie responded slowly to a combination of medications and therapy aimed at understanding the development of their obsessive thoughts and compulsive ritualistic actions. I first tried minor tranquilizers on them, to no avail, but found that an antidepressant was moderately effective in reducing some of their compulsive activities.

Psychotherapy consisted of helping them to understand their behavior as being caricatures of their personality structures. I asked them to verbalize their feelings in relation to current life events and pointed out several mental defense mechanisms (*see* chapter eleven) they were using. As they slowly recognized these, their symptoms gradually subsided. Bill returned to school, and Charlie's work and relationship with his wife improved.

Another special type of anxiety is a phobia, which is a sensation of panic when confronted with a particular situation, place, or object that rationally is known not to be a source of danger. Most women can't stand spiders, cockroaches, or mice. Many men are overly repulsed by snakes. Phobias have many fancy Greek or Latin names such as *acrophobia,* "fear of heights"; *pyrophobia,* "fear of fire"; *agoraphobia,* "fear of being alone in public or of wide open spaces or crowds"; and *nyctophobia,* "fear of darkness." Other common phobias include fear of dirt, germs, water, strangers, and animals. There are literally hundreds of other less well-known phobias.

Some years ago I saw a middle-aged man suffering from

an elevator phobia, a form of a *claustrophobia,* "fear of enclosed places." He was highly motivated to seek therapy because his job required him to visit clients in offices on high floors in many very tall buildings. For years he had been quite happy to use the stairs, but with increasing age he wanted to use an elevator, but couldn't.

In therapy I started by making him close his eyes and imagining himself stepping into an open elevator and hopping out again. Then he imagined himself wanting to go up just one floor, which took only a few seconds. At last he was gradually able to imagine himself ascending many floors.

The next stage was for him to actually do it, but for me to go with him. We went together to the elevator right outside my office, and we agreed to go up just one floor. With much anxiety he was able to do this, because I was with him, but he extracted a promise from me that we would walk back to my office via the stairs. The next week we increased the number of floors, and he was able to travel with me in both directions. Finally he tried just one floor by himself, then two, then several, and when I last saw him, he announced triumphantly that he had made it to the top of the World Trade Center and had thoroughly enjoyed the view!

I recently saw Claudia, a young married woman who suffered from agoraphobia, the fear of being alone in crowds. She worked in New York City, but lived outside the city. She therefore had to take the train every morning, but in the rush hour it was so packed that she often could not get a seat. She didn't mind standing herself, but was absolutely panicked when she saw no seats available and many other people standing between the seats and crowding the doorways. She especially hated the last portion of the trip in which the train traveled through a tunnel. The combination of the crowded train and the tunnel panicked her. She had never been stuck in the tunnel, but was terrified that one day she might be and would be unable to escape from the crowd. She could tolerate driving in a private automobile, through a road tunnel, but the use of the New York City subway would have been impossible.

A phobic person exposed to his own specific phobic object or situation suffers from intense irrational anxiety with such symptoms as nausea; tremors; sweating; fatigue; palpitations; faintness; diarrhea; and hyperventilation, which is increased depth and rate of breathing. If the sufferer avoids the phobic situation, the generalized anxiety of which it is a part is significantly reduced, but it could result in a major disruption of social or job responsibilities.

One theory of phobias is that they are caused by defensive displacement (*see* chapter eleven) in which the generalized anxiety is placed on one phobic object or situation. The patient avoids the anxiety by staying away from the situation. He manages his fear by unconsciously specifying and avoiding it.

Another dynamic of phobias is that of "secondary gain." For example, Claudia's primary gain was reducing her generalized anxiety by developing a specific phobia and then avoiding her phobic object (the crowded trains). Her secondary gain was increased concern and attention from her husband, parents, friends, and physician, which satisfied some dependency needs. When these were pointed out to her, she began the process of recovery. Tranquilizers helped her a little, especially in the early stages when she boldly began taking the train again. She only needed these for a few weeks, until with increasing practice she was able to take the trip without discomfort, first with her husband and eventually alone.

Hypnosis or hypnotherapy, especially if used more than once over a period of a few weeks, has proven to cure some phobias. If used, it should *only* be administered by a physician or other fully qualified and ethical professional. Do *not* go to a hypnotist stage performer!

Some doctors have given patients a written, guaranteed "safety pass," which when carried, assures them of a safe journey in a train, airplane, or even an elevator. One doctor bet his phobic homebound patient $1,000 that he would not die if he left his home and came to his office. The doctor could not lose. If the patient made it safely, the doctor won his bet. If the patient had died, he would not have been able to collect! The patient made it. The doctor forgave the debt. Therapy was successful!

I don't just throw in verses of Scripture haphazardly, but one that I have found especially helpful for phobics is: "What time I am afraid, I will trust in thee" (Psalms 56:3).

Finally we come to another category of disturbing thoughts collectively known as paranoia. The word *paranoia,* derived from the ancient Greek, in modern colloquial terms means "to be out of one's mind." The essential problem is a distortion in thinking that is characterized by a delusion. In extreme cases paranoid delusions can lead to a psychosis, as experienced by Mark (*see* chapter five). However, many paranoids are not psychotic in behavior, even though they do have a reality contact loss with regard to their particular delusion. Very often, with the exception of this delusion, all other thinking, feelings, and behavior can be otherwise normal.

A delusion is a false belief or idea having two essential factors: the belief is a disorder of judgment not consistent with the objective facts of reality; and it is fixed and not changeable by any influence of logic, common sense, reason, persuasion, rational explanation, or even by the demonstration of the objective, real facts.

A delusion can be of persecution, a belief that others are out to harm the patient, of reference, that others are looking at him or talking about him; of grandeur, that he believes he is some famous person; of influence, that others can read his mind or that he is getting personal messages from the TV or radio; or of the body, that he is seriously ill, when in fact he is in good physical health.

Mrs. Giles saw me several months ago, complaining that her husband was having an affair with his secretary. Her delusion had developed out of the real fact that, for business reasons, the previous year they had had to work late at the office on several occasions and had had to be in communcation with each other by telephone several evenings and weekends. Her false belief was further strengthened by her husband's reduced sexual attention to her.

I requested that Mr. Giles see me at least once, which he was anxious to do. He assured me that there was absolutely no truth to his wife's allegations. Whereas his secretary was indeed younger and attractive, he had no interest in her sexually. Even if he had, she was engaged to be married soon, and he knew that she would have rejected him had he made any advances toward her. Their relationship was friendly, but professional. His lack of interest in his wife he explained as being partly that her recent weight gain turned him off and partly that business difficulties had caused him such anxiety as to reduce his normal sex drive.

Mrs. Giles's paranoia progressed, over a period of several months, through many innocent incidents or comments in their homelife, which added more and more erroneous "evidence" to her delusional belief system. This system became highly developed, with a great deal of internal logical consistency. Her initial misinterpretation of events led to a whole series of complex rationalizations, each one leading into the next.

She became obsessed with her husband's infidelity, thought about it continually, yet was otherwise able to conduct her personal domestic responsibilities and her interpersonal relationships quite normally.

Questioning her history closely revealed some partially explanatory facts to account for her condition. As a child, her parents had expressed love for her, but also beat her harshly and inconsistently for misbehavior. She never knew where she stood with them and thereby never accurately learned the principles of reward and punishment.

She also confessed that she had the previous year met a former lover whom she had not seen since her marriage. She admitted to the reemergence of romantic feelings toward him, which were troublesome to her conscience. As a result these emotionally unacceptable impulses were rejected in her mind, and by the unconscious process called *projection* (*see* chapter eleven), she had attributed them to her husband.

Third, her recent weight gain had lowered her self-esteem, and being unable to accept her husband's diminished sexual drive for her, she led herself into the false belief that it had been caused by the secretary, rather than by herself.

I knew that none of these factors would convince Mrs. Giles of her delusion, but over several months, she came to trust me because I was not rejecting of her point of view. As I let her talk her troubles out I became the one person in her life whom she could talk to without fear of argument or rejection. I had to tread a very fine line with her, neither actually accepting or challenging unrealistic beliefs.

Had her delusion led to such hostility toward her husband that she had threatened physical violence, she would have needed to be hospitalized. Fortunately this never happened, and the use of a major tranquilizer in moderate doses gradually reduced her anxiety, anger, and the frequency of her delusional thoughts. Although she remained a very suspicious person, her specific delusion about her husband gradually abated sufficiently for them to live together in reasonable harmony.

Questions

1. Do you sometimes get unwanted thoughts that are contrary to your conscious moral, ethical, or spiritual prin-

ciples? If so, how do you handle them? Does practicing suppression help? Would it help to follow Paul's advice in Philippians 4:8?

2. Do you know anyone suffering from obsessions or compulsions, secular or religious? How would you attempt to counsel a Christian friend with such a problem? Share any experiences you have had in these areas.

3. Think and pray about Paul's admonition to us to be "Casting down imaginations . . . and bringing into captivity every thought to the obedience of Christ" (2 Corinthians 10:5). How does this verse apply to you personally, and to the problem of unwanted or obsessional thoughts in general?

4. Have you experienced a phobia or some similar form of acute anxiety? Psalms 56:3 was quoted in this chapter. Can you think of other verses exhorting the believer to "fear not," in either the Old or New Testaments? Share with others.

5. How would you cope with a loved one suffering from paranoid delusions? How could you encourage him to live in the truth? Could Paul's encouragement to be ". . . speaking the truth in love . . ." (Ephesians 4:15) help him? If so, in what way?

For Further Study

Backus, William, and Chapian, Marie. *Telling Yourself the Truth*. Minneapolis, Minn.: Bethany House, 1980.

Koheut, H. *The Analysis of the Self*. New York: International University Press, 1971.

LaHaye, Tim. *The Battle for the Mind*. Old Tappan, N.J.: Fleming H. Revell, 1980.

7

"I'm So Guilty, I Must Have Lost My Salvation"
True and False Guilt and the Unpardonable Sin

Beth had been an outstanding member of her church and a leader in her local community, until a couple of problems began to plague her life. Her husband was laid off from his job, so family finances suffered severely. Around the same time her elderly widowed mother also had had to be permanently confined to a nursing home.

Her mother became increasingly demanding that Beth visit her daily and spend many hours with her, which took away time she preferred to spend with her home and family. In an effort to keep food on the table, Beth had started shoplifting in a local supermarket and was eventually caught. Within days of her apprehension for stealing, she was driving one of her children to summer camp when her mother had a massive stroke and died. Beth became so distraught that she went to her pastor for counseling, saying she felt she must have committed the unpardonable sin. He sent her immediately to me.

"I'm so guilty, I must have lost my salvation," Beth started. "How can God forgive me? I've made a mess of my life. I can't look my friends in the eye anymore. I've dis-

that we are dust . . . the mercy of the Lord is from everlasting to everlasting. . .' (*see* Psalms 103).

"Of course the New Testament also has many references to God's mercy and forgiveness in Christ. His death on the cross made possible our total cleansing from sin. When we repent, that restores complete fellowship between God and man and results in complete peace within. This is how God has provided the very best psychotherapy or healing. Yet there is nothing magical about it—supernatural, yes; but magical, no. And although the believer cannot understand or scientifically measure divine healing, he *can* experience it through repentance.

"John, the apostle of love said, 'If we say that we have no sin, we deceive ourselves, and the truth is not in us. If we confess our sins, he is faithful and just to forgive us our sins and to cleanse us from all unrighteousness.' [1 John 1:8, 9]. Jesus Himself said, 'They that are whole have no need of a physician, but they that are sick: I came not to call the righteous, but sinners to repentance' " [Mark 2:17].

"I believe all that you've said," said Beth, "but I've still got this court appearance coming up."

"Yes, I know," I replied. "You still have to face the natural or human consequences of your actions, but you can even trust the Lord for that. We will all pray for you that God will not only forgive you for your sins of stealing, but also in His mercy make your human punishment bearable and without too much in the way of personal or social repercussions. I will pray with you that God will bring to pass what He wants for you in accordance with both His justice and His mercy."

"Thank you," Beth said appreciatively. "Now I feel a peace and know I've been forgiven through Christ's shed blood. So I guess I'll just try to trust God for the outcome of the legal proceedings. Next week can we talk about false guilt? I'm not really sure what that is."

She left considerably relieved by our discussion and by the passages of Scripture we'd studied together. I also closed our session with a brief prayer, which reassured her that God was in overall control of every detail of her life.

The next week she returned to say that a date had been fixed for her court appearance, but that she felt a strange sense of peace about it. She was still feeling guilty however about the last few days of her mother's life.

"Beth," I began, "the guilt feelings you have about your mother are largely a form of false guilt. Let me explain what that means.

"False guilt is either exaggerated or unnecessary guilt. It is merely a feeling, not an intellectual conviction of wrong-doing. It results from your cultural upbringing, social ideals, fear of taboos, or concern at losing the love of others. It results from the judgments of man, whereas true guilt is the genuine consciousness of having betrayed an authentic standard and as such results in the judgment of God.

"Take for example your guilty feelings about your mother. From your earliest years you were brought up to love and respect her, and since she had provided for you when you were young, you developed the conviction that you should provide for her in her old age. She imposed upon your developing conscience very rigid standards of right and wrong and very high expectations of your standards of behavior and achievements.

"She also probably imposed somewhat excessive punishment on you as a child and gave you too little praise, thanks, encouragements, congratulations, or appreciation. She was never satisfied and consequently caused you to grow up with a deep sense of inadequacy and even failure, so that you developed a permanent overburdening cloud of guilty feelings and inferiority. This has led you as an adult to feel insecure, low in self-esteem, blameworthy, deserving of punishment, pessimistic, and unworthy.

"You did all you could do for your mother. As it was, you deprived your family of your time and energies to be with her at the end. It was just an unexpected coincidence that she died the day you were away. But, remember, God is in control. He allowed that to happen when it did for a purpose—possibly many purposes, at least one of which was to enable you to resolve in your heart and mind this whole burden of false guilt you've been bearing for so many years."

"I'm beginning to understand," said Beth. "But now how do I actually get rid of my false guilt feelings?"

"Well, first of all," I replied. "What you do *not* need to do is to confess and repent. Since you did all you could for your mother, you did not sin. You have nothing to be truly guilty about, and therefore there is nothing that God can forgive you for.

"You need to think through what I have already said about the origins of false guilt. You need to understand and evaluate your feelings for what they really are. Self-condemnation is not your prerogative. God only is your judge. Try to learn that your false guilt feelings are the product of your rigid upbringing and unrealistic parental expectations.

"From now on live in response to the power of the Spirit within you, and don't think that you can either please God or reduce your sense of guilt by trying to be perfect. God expects us to live holy lives, to put His will first in our decisions and actions. He does not expect sinless perfection. If that were even possible, we would have no need of a redeeming Savior.

"Real sins are forgiven by God after repentance. We only need to confess and repent once. A second confession of the same sin would mean that you have not trusted in God's forgiveness the first time. You also cannot earn forgiveness by good works. Good works follow assurance of salvation as an act of gratitude and worship to God for what He has done for us in redemption. But they can never earn salvation. Only faith in Christ's shed blood can. Failure to understand this basic truth of the Gospel can lead Christians to live defeated lives and suffer the misery of false guilt, leading to worry, depression, loss of inner peace, and a sense of separation from God.

"Paul spelled this out very specifically for us. In his letter to the Christians in Galatia, he admonished them for their legalism and perfectionism. They were teaching the heresy that good works—or keeping the law—were necessary to supplement the redemptive work of Christ in salvation. He wrote, '... Received ye the Spirit by the works of the law, or by the hearing of faith? Are ye so foolish? having begun in the Spirit, are ye now made perfect by the flesh?' [Galatians 3:2, 3]. To the Romans he wrote, '... by the deeds of the law there shall no flesh be justified in his sight. . .' [Romans 3:20] and to the Colossians, 'And ye are complete in him, which is the head of all principality and power' [Colossians 2:10].

"Thank you," Beth said, "I'll work on what you've said. Next time, though, I'd like to find out about the unpardonable sin."

She returned two weeks later, after her court appearance, looking much relieved. "What happened?" I asked.

"Well, I pleaded guilty," she began, "and the judge asked me if I would like to confess to all the stealing I had done. I totaled it up, and it came to about one hundred and twenty dollars worth of groceries. He asked me if I would accept his judgment or be referred to a higher court. I wanted to get it all over with, so I said I'd accept his judgment. He was very merciful to me. He fined me one hundred and twenty dollars, to be paid to the court, and ordered me to repay another one hundred and twenty dollars to the supermarket. Then he put me on probation for a year. It could have been a lot worse. I'm really grateful to God. Oh, and by the way, Doug's just got a new job.

"So now what about the unpardonable sin?" she asked.

"First of all I'm glad your court case turned out the way it did," I replied. "God was truly merciful in response to our prayers. And please tell Doug that I'm very happy about his new job."

"Now with regard to the unpardonable sin: The most important thing to remember is that it doesn't exist—at least for a Christian. It is possible of course for an unbeliever to commit it, but I'm not sure if I've ever met such a person. I've seen several Christians in my practice who say they fear that they have committed it. Without exception they have all been truly born-again believers who were once certain of their salvation, but now have doubts. I have never heard a pagan express this fear, mainly because such a person does not know what the unpardonable sin is. This fear in Christians is not a spiritual matter. It is a psychological matter. It is a form of obsessive thinking seen in people suffering from acute anxiety, internal depression, or schizophrenia.

"The twelfth chapter of Matthew tells of the Lord healing a blind and dumb man possessed with a devil. The Pharisees, when they heard about it, said He had done it, '. . . by Beelzebub the prince of the devils' [Matthew 12:24]. They therefore ascribed to the devil the work of the Spirit of God. This, and only this, according to the entire Bible, is the one sin that cannot be pardoned.

"Jesus states this to them explicitly in His reply: '. . .All manner of sin and blasphemy shall be forgiven unto men: but the blasphemy against the Holy Ghost shall not be forgiven unto men. And whosoever speaketh a word against the Son of man, it shall be forgiven him: but whosoever speaketh against the Holy Ghost, it shall not be forgiven him, neither in this world, neither in the world to come' [Matthew 12:31, 32; *see also* Mark 3:28, 29; Luke 12:10].

"This sin is unpardonable because the conviction of sin is the work of the Holy Spirit. When He is blasphemed this way, He completely withdraws, so that conviction cannot take place. Removal of the Spirit causes the blasphemer to care no more. He goes, lost, to eternity, with no concern or care.

"No person who is born of the Spirit could commit the unpardonable sin, because as long as the Spirit is still working in a person's heart and mind, He is still there. If someone *does* have a concern that he might have committed this sin, he could not have. The Spirit has given him that conviction, so the Christian who experiences anxiety, depression, or

guilt about this issue can know that the Spirit has not left
him and that he is still saved. Once saved, always saved. Remember that once you are saved, '. . . greater is he that is in
you [the Holy Spirit], than he that is in the world [Satan]' [1
John 4:4].

"Two well-known passages in Hebrews have a bearing on
this subject: 'For it is impossible for those who were once
enlightened . . . If they shall fall away, to renew them again
unto repentance . . .' [Hebrews 6:4, 6]. Also later, 'For if we
sin wilfully after that we have received the knowledge of
the truth, there remaineth no more sacrifice for sins. . .' [He-
brews 10:26].

"These passages refer to those who profess belief, but stop
short of a commitment to a saving faith in Christ, after ad-
vancing to the very threshold of salvation. Neither passage
states that the people referred to were truly born again or
thoroughly committed believers. They merely professed to
be interested, even up to the point of repentance, but were
never fully saved."

"Okay. I guess I'm not in that category," said Beth finally.
"But I'll remember your points, to help others in doubt."

"Good," I concluded. "Remember the positive Scriptures.
The truly saved person is eternally secure, as Jesus said: '. . .
He that heareth my word, and believeth on him that sent
me, hath everlasting life, and shall not come into condem-
nation; but is passed from death unto life' [John 5:24]. Also
later He said: 'My sheep hear my voice, and I know them,
and they follow me: And I give unto them eternal life; and
they shall never perish, neither shall any man pluck them
out of my hand' " [John 10:27, 28].

QUESTIONS

1. Discuss true guilt and the biblical provisions for dealing with it. Do you have any residual true guilt? Think and
pray about any hindrance to forgiveness.

2. Is any unrepented sin blocking your peace of forgiveness? If so, what should you do about it? If God can forgive you, can you forgive yourself? If not, share and discuss this with a mature Christian friend.

3. Are you aware of any false guilt you have experienced? If so, what makes it false rather than true guilt? Discuss these feelings with other mature Christians. Talk them through to regain peace with God.

4. Pray about for yourself, and discuss with others, the verses on guilt and forgiveness quoted in this chapter: Exodus 20:15; Isaiah 1:18, 57:20, 21; Psalms 103; 1 John 1:8, 9; Mark 2:17; Galatians 3:2, 3; Romans 3:20.

5. Discuss with others how to counsel a Christian who has the false belief that he or she has committed the unpardonable sin. Think and pray about the quoted verses: Matthew 12:24, 31, 32: Mark 3:28; Luke 12:10; 1 John 4:4; Hebrews 6:4, 6, 10:26; John 5:24, 10:27, 28.

FOR FURTHER STUDY

Augsburger, David. *The Freedom of Forgiveness.* Chicago: Moody Press, 1970.

Hallesby, O. *Conscience.* Downers Grove, Ill.: Inter Varsity, 1950.

Justice, William G. *Guilt: The Source and Solution.* Wheaton, Ill.: Tyndale, 1981.

Lindsey, Hal, and Carlson, C. C. *The Guilt Trip.* Grand Rapids, Mich.: Zondervan, 1973.

Narramore, Bruce, and Counts, Bill. *Freedom From Guilt.* Eugene, Ore.; Harvest House, 1976.

Tournier, Paul. *Guilt and Grace.* New York: Harper & Row, 1962.

8

"I Feel So Uptight and Panicky"
Anxiety and Stress

Anxiety is not only by far the commonest symptom complained of in a psychiatrist's office, it is also the most frequently observed emotion in society as a whole in twentieth-century civilization. We live in an age of anxiety.

David is a bright, well-educated young man, a second-generation American, who was having difficulties in his final year working for his Ph.D.

His father, the struggling but eventually successful son of central European immigrants, and his domineering, demanding, but overprotective mother ruled with rigid authority and highly verbalized expectations in the home in which David and his siblings were raised through the sixties and seventies.

All went well through high school, college, and the early years of graduate school. Shortly before I saw David he had begun work on his Ph.D. dissertation, and his original proposal had not been acceptable to his professor. That man had had a high regard for David and felt that he could produce something better. In attempting to redo his proposal, David found that fresh ideas failed to come, his deadline date was fast approaching, and he began to get panic attacks, which further reduced his ability to think constructively.

A second cause for anxiety, not so acute, but more persistent, was his concern about the prospects for employment after getting his degree. Unemployed Ph.D.s were a dime a dozen, many of them having to settle for jobs for which they were overqualified. He was hoping to get married after graduation, and a well-paying job right away was essential. Also his parents persisted in expressing high expectations for his future, putting additional stress on him.

"David," I said, "let's deal with the second problem first. First we'll deal with your generalized anxiety; then we can devote our efforts to dealing with the panic attacks.

"I appreciate your fears about the bad job market, but that's at least a year in the future. There's no point worrying about something that might never happen. Your parents' anxiety for you is their problem, not yours. At present it seems that the worst that could happen to you might be the need to postpone your marriage a few months but that might not even be necessary. I'm sure your fiancée would understand and respect you if you decided to wait until you got a good job worthy of your education.

"Your primary responsibility right now is to get on with your thesis. We can talk some more about your generalized anxiety some other time. Meanwhile a temporary course of a minor tranquilizer would just take the edge off that, so that you would feel calmer during the day. Take the fewest you need, and don't use them for more than a month or two."

"Now I'm more concerned about the panic attacks, because they are much more seriously disruptive to your ability to think clearly and function effectively. See if you can describe one for me, say the most recent one you had."

"Well, they're so sudden," David started. "Like last Friday evening I was struggling with some new ideas for my thesis when I began thinking about how behind schedule I was. Suddenly it was as if I'd been hit by some unseen force. It started with just a general feeling of acute tension; you know, sort of very uptight, unable to relax. I couldn't concentrate on my work anymore, and I became aware of a sense of fear, but there was nothing to be afraid of, except my schedule problem. It gradually got worse. I felt a terrifying sense of dread, of impending doom or destruction, of utter helplessness. I felt physically weak, terribly fatigued, trembling as if I was going to faint, and I got goose bumps all over my arms and legs. I broke out in a cold sweat, yet my face seemed hot and flushed. My stomach felt all in knots. My heart pumped fast, and I had a pain across the front of my chest. I thought at first that I was having a heart attack. I also felt a sense of suffocation, of difficulty breathing, yet I realized that I was actually breathing very fast. I had an urgent need to go to the bathroom, even though I had just been."

"What happened then?" I asked.

"It got worse. I thought I was dying. I felt light-headed, dizzy, and could feel a sharp headache coming on. My mind became confused; my room began to look unfamiliar, even unreal; and I started to feel, well, kind of detached between mind and body. I felt I wanted to vomit, but all I did was retch. My sister called, but I couldn't even speak to her coherently. I said I'd call her back tomorrow, and then I noticed that I was shaking and twitching all over. I thought: *I'm going crazy!*"

"And then?" I questioned.

"Well, I gobbled down three or four Valiums and took a slug of vodka I usually just keep for friends. I turned out the lights and lay on the bed. I'm not used to alcohol, so the vodka worked very quickly. I calmed down pretty soon and eventually went off to sleep still fully dressed.

"I woke up on Saturday morning with quite a hangover-type headache, but otherwise I was fine. In fact after two aspirins, a couple of cups of strong coffee, and a good breakfast, I was able to get back to work. I called my sister and apologized for being so irritable and impatient the previous evening. She was very sympathetic and understanding."

"How many of these attacks have you had?"

"Only about five or six, but the last one was the worst," David responded. "I've got to get over them, or I'll end up in a hospital, ruin my career, possibly lose my fiancée, even lose my mind."

"Not that bad, David," I replied. "We've got some answers to your problem, fairly recently discovered, but usually very effective according to several recent clinical studies."

"Studies?" he queried. "You mean, like, I could be some sort of human guinea pig?"

"No," I reassured him, "others have gone before. Let me briefly explain what I have in mind.

"For years the medical profession assumed that tranquilizers were the most effective—indeed the only—chemical treatment for acute anxiety attacks, but they at best merely mask the symptoms—which is better than nothing—but they do not control the panic attacks. Now we have discovered something new, even somewhat paradoxical. Antidepressant medications have been found, almost by accident, to be very effective in reducing your kind of panic symptoms. I say *paradoxical* because antidepressants are normally considered to be 'up' type drugs, in other words, the very opposite that someone already 'hyper' should have. But the results of several tests quite recently have shown that antidepressant medications are very effective in reducing both the symptoms and frequency of panic attacks. No one yet fully understands how or why they work or the way they do, but antidepressants seem to be effective in reducing acute anxiety such as you have experienced."

I gave him a brief account of the theory of neurotransmitters described in chapters three and eight.

"Well, you're the doctor," David said—a statement that frequently puts *me* into a state of anxiety! In spite of all the professional training and many years of experience I have had, I'm *very* well aware that I am not infallible.

"Okay, David," I replied. "But I'm not perfect. I can't predict the future, and I've made my fair share of mistakes. However, on the basis of what I presently know and have seen to affect others, I suggest you give these a try, at least for a couple of months."

I gave him two prescriptions, one for a fairly strong antidepressant, as a preventive for his panic attacks, and the other for a relatively mild tranquilizer for his generalized anxiety.

He returned the following week. He initially looked no different as he walked in from the waiting room, but once we started to talk, he expressed some slight improvements.

"Well, I have to admit that I haven't had another of those terrible panic attacks," he started, "which I suppose means that the meds are working, at least so far."

"Good," I said. "Stick with them for the immediate future. If you do, my prediction is that you'll be rid of the acute episodes."

"Yeah, but for how long?" David appropriately asked.

"Probably as long as you are taking the antidepressants; but once you're over your academic, personal, and employment crises, I can confidently predict that you won't need them anymore. Imagine yourself with a Ph.D., a great job, with prospects for good career advancement, happily married, with a family on the way. Do you think you'll need any more dumb pills or capsules then?"

"Well, I sure hope not," David said.

"Please don't worry," I reassured him. "I've seen many others with far worse symptoms than yours. They virtually all recover totally, given time and motivation. Now please remember, all of this is not something magical. It's a matter of science, medicine, and logical reasoning, albeit based on our very limited knowledge or understanding.

"However, there is this additional factor. Part of your psychological improvement is dependent on a trusting relationship with either me or any other therapist or counselor with whom you can develop a committed relationship."

David was soon able to see me less frequently and as of this writing has sucessfully completed his dissertation. His professor is confident that he will find a good job, and wedding plans are not being postponed. He takes no more tranquilizers, but feels more secure keeping a small supply of the antidepressants "just in case." I doubt if he will ever again need them.

Stress is by far the most common external cause of anxiety that results in internal chemical changes that produce symptoms such as David's. Two parts of the brain, the hypothalamus and the limbic system, were especially affected by his biochemical imbalance and resulted in the experiences he suffered.

The external factors that caused David's stress included his fear of failure, his professor's initial disappointment in him, the pressure of wanting to please his parents, the deadline time drawing close, and his desire not to have to postpone his wedding.

We all experience stress from time to time. Actually, life would be rather boring without some of it, but too much, especially all at once, causes anxiety. The stresses and strains of modern-day urban living, with its noise and bustle, crowds and schedules, appointments and responsibilities, priorities and conflicts all contribute to the anxiety of daily life. The poor worry about where the next meal is coming from; the rich agonize over how their investments are affected by the fluctuations in the national and world economy; the middle class struggle with cash flow and the monthly budget.

Stress is the wear and tear of life, and eventually the stress of just living may become too much. A few common sense practices can enable life to be less stressful and more enjoyable. Here's what I personally do to achieve this, and recommend that you try:

1. *Accept reality.* Live within the limits of your own abilities. Change what you can, but don't get frustrated by the unchangeable. Resentment, bitterness, hostility, jealousy, or anger will give you ulcers or high blood pressure.

2. *Face your fears.* Think of what is the worst that could happen and what you would do if it did. Then figure what the chances are; they're usually pretty small. Ninety-nine percent of what you're afraid of will never happen.

3. *Quit self-pity.* Whenever you catch yourself having pessimistic, morbid, depressing, or self-destructive thoughts, deliberately replace them with more positive, hopeful ones. Think of something pleasurable you're anticipating or some achievement you're striving for.

4. *Laugh at yourself.* Your petty problems are nothing compared with the suffering of others. Enjoy the little things of life. Give thanks for all your blessings.

5. *Relax regularly.* Work hard, but always arrange for some fun activity to look foward to in the near future, preferably with others. Avoid overeating, alcohol, or drugs. They are very poor methods of escape. (*See* chapter fourteen.)

6. *Sleep well.* Seven hours minimum for adults, eight for adolescents and children. Avoid going to bed anxious, depressed, or angry if at all possible. Forget the day's problems. Don't use sleep medications regularly, only when prescribed by your doctor for special, brief periods.

7. *Discuss your problems.* Get them off your chest. Share them with your spouse, a close family member,

trusted friend, or pastor. At work be brave enough to level with the boss. Don't be too proud to have a few sessions with a psychiatrist or counselor.

8. *Take breaks regularly.* Get away from the children with your spouse one evening every week and one weekend every three months. Don't be afraid to ask a good friend or grandparents to take care of the kids; they've probably been waiting for you to ask! Have a minimum of two weeks of vacation every year away from your hometown. (Even if it's only ten miles away!)

9. *Keep physically fit.* Take plenty of vigorous exercise regularly (*see* chapter fourteen). Keep your weight to within five pounds of normal for your height. Have medical and dental checkups regularly as recommended.

10. *Worship the Lord.* Attend church regularly. Make your faith personal. Believe it. Live it. Christians should enjoy plenty of fellowship and budget time for disciplined private prayer and Bible study. King David said, "The Lord is my light and my salvation; whom shall I fear? the Lord is the strength of my life; of whom shall I be afraid?" (Psalms 27:1). Jesus said, "Let not your heart be troubled; ye believe in God, believe also in me" (John 14:1). He also said, "Peace I leave with you, my peace I give unto you. . . . Let not your heart be troubled, neither let it be afraid" (John 14:27). Paul said, "Be careful for nothing; but in every thing by prayer and supplication with thanksgiving let your requests be made known unto God. And the peace of God, which passeth all understanding, shall keep your hearts and *minds* through Christ Jesus" (Philippians 4:6, 7, *italics added*).

Questions

1. What is the worst experience of anxiety that you have ever had? Share with others how it was resolved by yourself, by outside help, by natural change of circumstances, or by divine intervention. Was your faith shaken or enhanced by it?

2. What is your attitude toward taking minor tranquilizers for anxiety? Is it wrong for a Christian to take them even if prescribed by a physician? How would you counsel a Christian with anxiety who refused to take such medications?

3. Discuss in your group the ten recommendations in this chapter for reducing stress. Share examples of how you have tried some of these for yourself. Which ones work for you, and which ones do not?

4. Contemplate before the Lord and apply to your own life the verses quoted in this chapter: Psalms 27:1; John 14:1, 27; Philippians 4:6, 7. Think of several other verses that encourage us to calm down, to fear less, and to trust the Lord more.

For Further Study

Collins, Gary R. *Calm Down.* 2nd ed. Santa Ana, Calif.: Vision House, 1982.

Green, Bernard, and Schwarz, Ted. *Goodbye, Blues.* New York: McGraw-Hill, 1981.

May, Rollo. *The Meaning of Anxiety.* New York: Norton, 1977.

Osgood, Don. *Thirty Days to a Less Stressful You.* Chappaqua, N.Y.: Christian Herald, 1980.

Selye, Hans. *Stress Without Distress.* New York: Harper & Row, 1974.

9

"It Sounds Too Good to Be True"

Mood Swings: Ecstasy or Despair

Mrs. Alvarez was highly agitated as she came into my office. She began talking before she even sat down.

"I've come, not for myself, but about my son, Julio. Right now he's behaving crazy. I can't keep up with him. He never stops talking—to me, his sister, or on the telephone. He seems to stay up all night, making phone calls or swinging to his rock music. He spends money on things he doesn't need. He even gives it to beggars. It's as if he's on drugs, but he swears he isn't. I've looked, but I couldn't find any alcohol or pot, or even smell any. He never seems to sleep.

"It's impossible to talk sensibly to him. He's actually unable to stick to one subject at a time. His mind flits from one topic to another, completely illogically. He keeps on interrupting and always totally dominates any conversation. He seems in such a high mood all the time, elated, ecstatic, as if something wonderful had just happened to him, but nothing has."

"How long has he been like this?" I asked.

"About three or four days, but that's as much as we can take. He's driving us all crazy."

"What was he like before this came on, say a week or ten days ago?"

"The very opposite. He was depressed, very quiet, and withdrawn. We could hardly get a word out of him."

"And how long was he depressed?" I questioned.

"Several weeks, but back a few months ago he was high again for a few days, like now."

"How long have these moods swings been going on?" I queried. "And how frequently do they recur?"

"Well, I guess the first I remember was when he lost his first job. After graduating from high school, he decided he didn't want to go to college, but got a good job in construction. He joined the union and was earning a good salary and was planning on getting married. Then everything seemed to go wrong.

"He began to become very moody, lost interest in his girl friend, and began saying he didn't feel like going to work. He stayed in his room, wouldn't eat meals I brought up for him, even mumbled something about he'd rather be dead.

"Then one day he suddenly seemed to change. It was as if he'd just won a million dollars. He went rushing off to work with a wild enthusiasm we'd never seen before. We were glad at first, but then a little fearful for him, wondering what was going to happen next.

"Our worst fears were soon realized. He got a ticket for speeding on his way to work and then got into a terrible argument with his boss, ending up in his taking a swing at him, and he got fired on the spot.

"From then on it has been downhill. It seems as if he's either very high or very low, about every few weeks. It's rare for him to be in the middle, normal, like his old self. He's had several jobs, all of which he has lost either because he has been too depressed to show up for work or so high that he gets fired for being either totally unreliable or belligerent."

"Has he had any treatment from any other doctor for these problems?" I asked.

"Yes, our family doctor has given him tranquilizers,

usually Valium, for his high moods and sometimes an anti-depressant if he gets depressed and asks for some."

"Mrs. Alvarez," I said. "Julio, from all you've said, is clearly suffering from a manic-depressive disorder for which there is a very effective treatment, lithium."

"What's lithium," she asked, "some wonder drug?"

"No, it's not a drug at all, it's just a simple salt, almost as simple as the common table salt you use at home. That's sodium chloride; this is lithium carbonate, a different form, but similar in general principle to a regular salt.

"Julio's condition essentially is caused by an imbalance in the brain cells between the simple but important elements sodium and potassium. We don't know how or why they get out of whack, but when they do, mood swings develop. Lithium helps to restore the right balance and thereby will control his mood swings and will restore him to living a normal life."

"Sounds too good to be true," she said. "But how can I get him to see you? He says he's feeling great and doesn't need a doctor or any kind of help."

"I'll tell you what," I responded. "Tell Julio you saw me and say that I have requested to see him. Say that I would need to see him as part of my efforts as a family counselor. I can really only confirm my diagnosis after talking with him face to face, but to get him here, tell him he could help the whole family if he came."

I did not have long to wait. As Mrs. Alvarez had predicted, he came down from the high within a few days and was responsive to coming with her to see me.

"Julio," I inquired, "has your mother explained to you about our talk together last week?"

"Yes," he replied. "She said you're a family counselor, but also a physician."

"Good," I said. "Then may I relate to you first as a physician?"

"Oh, yes," he said, "and I guess I feel now that I ought to get some medical help."

"Good. Then give me a summary of your mood-swing history for as far back as you can remember it."

"What do you mean 'mood swings'?" he asked.

"According to your mother, you've had up-and-down moods—that is, depression and what we call manic attacks—on and off for a few years now. Tell me about them from your own memory."

Julio's historical summary, which was brief and slightly evasive, even apologetic, almost exactly paralleled my recordings of the dates his mother had given me the previous week.

When he had finished, I said to him, "You know, Julio, I've got some bad news and some good news for you. The bad news is that you are suffering from a medical condition known as manic-depressive illness. But the good news is that you are *not* crazy; the condition is treatable; and best of all, if you cooperate, you can live a completely normal life from here on!"

"Sounds too good to be true," he echoed the earlier remark of his mother's. "But now what do I have to do?"

"Very simple," I said. "How much do you weigh?"

"About one hundred and sixty pounds. I had a complete annual physical exam last month."

"Any heart, kidney, liver, or thyroid problems?"

"Not any that I know of. My doctor says that I'm pretty physically fit."

"Okay. Take three of these capsules daily with meals and come to see me once a month for a blood test to ensure that the concentration of the lithium in your system is not either too low to be effective or so high as to be toxic."

"How long do I take them?" he appropriately asked.

"Possibly permanently," I responded. "Don't think of them as *treatment;* think of lithium as *prevention.* You're taking them to stabilize your mood, to prevent you in future from having high or low moods, manic or depressive attacks. At the very least take them for two years and possibly then we can try you for a period without them. Those two years will enable you to get yourself established in your work. With the 90 percent certainty of knowing you are going to be emotionally stable from now on, you can confidently begin to develop a lifelong career of your choice."

Julio has been on lithium for three years now. He is a foreman in his construction company, recently married, and since he started on lithium, he has had no more uncontrollable high or low mood swings.

"Want to try going off lithium for a while?" I asked him recently.

"No way!" he replied quickly. "No way I'd take the risk of losing my job, my wife, home, and happiness. If God chooses to work a life-changing miracle through a simple salt, I'm going to keep going His way!"

When a patient is a Christian, there are many passages of Scripture that can be of help. This is especially true when he is depressed and hurting. When he is high, however, he tends to be unable to be attentive to God's Word.

One of Job's comforters said, "When men are cast down, then thou shalt say, There is lifting up; and he shall save the humble person" (Job 22:29). David sang: "The righteous cry, and the Lord heareth, and delivereth them out of all their troubles. . . . He will regard the prayer of the destitute and not despise their prayer" (Psalms 34:17; 102:17). Isaiah said: ". . . Thou shalt weep no more: he will be very gracious unto thee at the voice of thy cry; when he shall hear it, he will answer thee" (Isaiah 30:19). To Israel He said, "When thou passest through the waters, I will be with thee; and through the rivers, they shall not overflow thee. . ." (Isaiah 43:2). The writer to the Hebrews said, "Now no chastening for the present seemeth to be joyous, but grievous: nevertheless afterward it yieldeth the peaceable fruit of righteousness unto them which are exercised thereby" (Hebrews 12:11).

Questions

1. Have you yourself, or do you know someone who has suffered from up-and-down moods? If so, how have you or they coped with it? Lithium carbonate is not a drug, but a salt. If you object to *drugs,* could you condone a *salt* as treatment for yourself or a loved one with this condition? Discuss your attitude toward the prescription of medications for any emotional disorders.

2. Do you think Julio's mania was demonic, psychological, medical, or partly all three? Whichever it was, where does God come in? What should be a Christian's attitude to each of these three causations of disease? Are there others? If so, what are they? Is there such a thing as a spiritual disease? If so, can you give an example? What should be done about it?

3. Pray about and apply to yourself the verses of Scripture quoted in this chapter: Job 22:29; Psalms 34:17, 102:17; Isaiah 30:19, 43:2; Hebrews 12:11.

For Further Study

Fieve, Ronald. *Moodswing.* New York: William Morrow, 1975.

10

"Help Me, I'm So Depressed"
External and Internal Depression

Not all depressions are of the up-and-down types that Julio experienced. The majority are composed of just the low component.

It is of course normal to be depressed at times, especially if some personal loss occurs, such as the death of a loved one, being fired from one's job, or failure to obtain something you wanted very much. Financial losses or deterioration in physical health or in a marital or premarital love relationship can also cause depression. This type is called reactive depression for that reason and is the result of external problems, outside the self. It is almost always of brief duration, like a normal grief or mourning period, gets better by itself, given a few weeks, and usually needs no medical treatment.

A far more serious type of depression is the internal sort, not caused by any external problems in life, but by a chemical imbalance in the brain, similar to that which causes anxiety (*see* chapter eight).

Harold came to see me several months ago, accompanied by his wife, Helen. He looked very sad and withdrawn and wanted his wife to do all the talking.

"We've been happily married for twenty-five years," she started. "He's got a secure, well-paying job, and our three children are all healthy and doing well in school. Even our parents are still in good health for their age. There's nothing whatever for us to be worried about, but over the last several months Harold has just simply been getting more and more depressed. Our family doctor has thoroughly checked him over, and there's nothing wrong physically. He suggested that Harold see you."

I turned to Harold, hoping for some account of how he felt. "See if you can describe your symptoms," I requested.

"I can't explain it," he began. "It's been getting worse over the last several months. I can't think of anything that happened that started it. We're all a healthy, happy family, except for me. I just feel down, sad for no reason I can think of. It's painful. I hate it. I just somehow feel discouraged, hopeless, and helpless. I feel isolated and lonely, even though I know I'm surrounded by loved ones. I often feel like crying for no reason. Sometimes I even wish I could just die."

"Any physical complaints?" I inquired.

"Well, yes, I guess I have to admit to some, but my doctor says I'm okay physically."

"That's good, but what have you actually experienced?"

"I haven't been sleeping well at night. It's hard at first to get to sleep, but the worst is waking up at three in the morning and not being able to go back to sleep."

"Anything else?"

"I've lost my appetite. No food seems to appeal to me, even though my wife in an excellent cook. Also I've been somewhat constipated recently. One of my colleagues at the office, who hadn't seen me for a month, said that I'd lost a lot of weight, but I haven't weighed myself. He also said that I looked fatigued and acted lethargic. I admit I've been feeling very apathetic on the job recently. Everything seems to have slowed down. I'm taking a long time making decisions and even longer acting on them. I feel kind of blah."

He then fell into a silence, so I turned to his wife. "Can you think of anything else, Helen?"

"Yes. He's sometimes quite uneasy, agitated, pacing the floor, wringing his hands, and easily irritated by the children. At other times he just sits for long periods, with his head drooping, and a mournful look on his face, with an occasional sob or sigh. Sometimes he actually cries.

"He talks very little, but when he does, he talks about how he's failed or done something wrong—even when he hasn't really. He feels guilt or shame over nothing. He thinks he's a failure. He's so gloomy. He used to have a good sense of self-esteem, but not anymore. He says he feels empty and worthless. He's preoccupied with morbid thoughts about himself. Frankly, he's become a little hard to live with recently; he's so withdrawn.

"Another thing," she went on. "There's no pleasure in his life. He doesn't enjoy anything anymore. He seems to find life dull and uninteresting.. He used to love playing golf or a rubber or two of bridge, but he hasn't played either for two months at least. His club friends are beginning to call me to find out if he's sick. One who noticed his weight loss asked me point-blank if he had cancer. He does complain of several minor aches and pains, but there's no real medical problem."

"How his relationship with you?" I asked.

"Well, I wasn't going to complain, but since you asked, that's one more problem. He's completely lost his sex drive. He used to come home every evening and give me a big hug and a long kiss. Now he's totally unresponsive. At first I feared he had a girl friend, but he reassured me it was his depression that was causing his lack of affection. He says that he's got no interest in having sex with me or anyone else. I've tried to encourage him, but he can barely keep his erection, let alone have intercourse."

"Well, Harold," I said, "You've come to the right place. I'm so sorry for you and your family that you didn't come a lot sooner. Don't reproach youself any more. You have a medical illness called *endogenous*—that means internal—depression. It's caused by a lack of adrenaline and other similar hormones in parts of your brain. Don't feel guilty. It's just as much a medical disease as the flu or acute appendicitis; and there's a medical cure for it. A few months on an antidepressant medication will get you over this."

"How soon will it begin to work?" he asked anxiously.

"Ten days to two weeks at the most, depending on how your body responds to it. I'll see you again next week, and if you are not already feeling better by then, it would be quite safe to increase the dosage. I'd rather not give you a nighttime sedative, because your insomnia will automatically get better as your depression lifts."

They were back a week later and both reported slight improvement. Harold certainly looked more lively.

"I think the pills are working a little," said Helen enthusiastically, "he's begun showing me some affection again!"

"How much longer should I take the pills, doctor?" Harold asked.

"Several months, please, Harold," I begged. "Don't be impatient. They don't work like aspirin, for an hour or two. They work over a period of days or weeks. If you quit the pills now, you'll be depressed again within a week. On the other hand, if you stick with them, we'll start gradually reducing the dosage after several weeks. Eventually, of course, you'll be able to discontinue them completely."

"Will this ever happen to me again?" he anxiously inquired.

"Maybe so, maybe not." I said. "Obviously we can't predict the future, but since this is the first such episode in your fifty years of life, the chances are that by the time the next one is due, you'll be with the Lord!" He laughed for the first time in a long while.

"There *is* a condition known as recurrent depression," I warned, "but if you should have a recurrence, come back to me at once, and we'll nip it in the bud. Don't go through weeks of suffering again, if there is a next time. As I said I'm hopeful there won't be a next time!"

I followed up with Harold, weekly at first and then

monthly, for about a year. He eventually got off his medication and has sent me a Christmas card every year since then. I've had five so far, and he's had no recurrence, so he's probably now fully recovered.

Three other types of depression must be mentioned, because as Christian friends we need to be able to recognize them so that we can be of help in advising how to obtain healing.

Three or four weeks after she had delivered her first baby, Sherry suddenly started experiencing feelings of inadequacy, anxiety, and *postpartum depression.* Discussion revealed apprehension about the new responsibility of motherhood and depression based on a feeling that she would be incapable of taking care of her child.

She recovered rapidly however, without medication, after I suggested that her mother come to stay with her family for a few weeks. With increased verbal support, affection, and practical help from her husband, and a lot of advice, teaching, and encouragement from her understanding mother, her depression and anxiety disappeared as her self-confidence grew.

Rather like Mark (*see* chapter five), who had a mental breakdown, I saw another man, rather older, who had somewhat similar symptoms of loss of contact with reality. His predominant symptom was depression—*psychotic depression,* which was associated with delusions, hallucinations, and a conspicuous thinking disorder. He was a serious suicidal risk and had to be immediately hospitalized to protect him from himself. He was placed on suicide observation twenty-four hours a day by the hospital staff and treated with antipsychotic medications.

As his reality contact was gradually restored, his depression lifted, and upon discharge from the hospital, I followed him on an outpatient basis for several months without recurrence. When he left town for a new job, I gave him the name of a psychiatrist in his new location, advising that he keep in touch with him.

Finally, it is quite common for women to become very depressed around the time of menopause. This is known as *involutional melancholia*. Milly was one such lady, who developed an acute agitated depression with insomnia when she first realized that her periods were no longer regular. Happily married for almost thirty years, Milly began developing delusional ideas that she was having an affair with a male neighbor she found attractive. She became obsessed with her own slightly overweight condition, menstrual changes, other bodily functions, and feelings of worthlessness, self-condemnation, guilt, and impending doom or death.

Milly became progressively worse over a period of a couple of weeks, and I had to recommend to her husband that she be hospitalized after she had taken an ineffective overdose of sleeping pills, leaving a note saying that she deserved to die for her sins. In the hospital, high doses of both antipsychotic and antidepressant medications failed to cure Milly, and it was eventually decided with her husband's consent that she should undergo a course of electroshock treatments. After a dozen of these, over a period of a month, she showed great improvement, was discharged from the hospital, and I am now seeing her every two weeks. She is doing well on a low maintenance dose of antidepressants.

Depressed patients always feel better through talking out the various real or imagined causes of their low mood. Psychotherapy for them consists mainly of being a patient listener. With the exception of psychotics, sufferers almost always leave with a sense of uplift if they have shared their sorrows with someone who cares.

Activity, both physical and mental, is also very helpful. I always strongly encourage depressed patients to make a special effort, however difficult initially, to become involved in worthy causes, especially ones that are committed to helping others in need. Caring for others helps take the mind off one's own concerns. Exercise also is very important (*see* chapter fifteen). I've never met a depressed jogger!

Finally, for the Christian who believes in the divine inspiration of the Bible, I have no hesitation in urging private prayer and Bible study. I frequently end my sessions with a depressed or anxious person with a brief prayer asking for healing and help from God for his or her specific problems.

Paul wrote to the Christians in Rome: "And we know that all things work together for good to them that love God, to them who are the called according to his purpose" (Romans 8:28). To the Corinthians he said, "Blessed be God . . . Who comforteth us in all our tribulation," and, ". . . he said unto me, My grace is sufficient for thee: for my strength is made perfect in weakness. . ." (2 Corinthians 1:3, 4; 12:9).

Jesus said, "Come unto me, all ye that labour and are heavy laden, and I will give you rest" (Matthew 11:28). At the Last Supper, He said, "If ye shall ask any thing in my name, I will do it" (John 14:14). Later He said, "I will not leave you comfortless: I will come to you" (John 14:18), and, ". . . ask, and ye shall receive, that your joy may be full" (John 16:24).

We have a prayer-answering God, a redeeming Savior, and a comforting Holy Spirit, who care, love, and give to meet all our needs.

Questions

1. Everyone has experienced at least a minor or temporary depression. What is the worst episode of depression you have experienced? Share the circumstances with your group. How did you cope with it?

2. Is anyone in your group depressed right now? Share some answers from your personal life and from the Scriptures. Discuss the many symptoms of depression mentioned

in this chapter. Explore to see if someone has some of these and may be depressed but does not realize it. What then should he or she do?

3. Do you agree that some depression could be of medical (biochemical) origin? If so, what should be done to treat it? If not, what would be a counseling and scriptural approach to alleviating the symptoms? Examine your own opinions to see if you are consistent and honest about your attitudes toward emotional problems.

4. What is your attitude toward suicide? What do you believe the Bible teaches about it? Can a suicide victim be eternally saved? If so, why? If not, why not? Discuss biblical evidences for your opinion.

5. Think, pray about, and apply to yourself the passages quoted in this chapter. Discuss them with others: Romans 8:28; 2 Corinthians 1:3, 4, 12:9; Matthew 11:28; John 14:14, 18, 16:24.

For Further Study

Barrett, Roger. *Depression: What It Is and What to Do About It.* Elgin, Ill.: David C. Cook, 1979.

Fraser, Sarah. *Living With Depression and Winning.* Wheaton, Ill.: Tyndale, 1975.

Kline, Nathan. *From Sad to Glad.* New York: Ballantine, 1981.

Lloyd-Jones, D. Martyn. *Spiritual Depression: Its Causes and Cure.* Grand Rapids, Mich.: Eerdmans, 1965.

Lowen, Alexander. *Depression and the Body.* Baltimore: Penguin, 1973.

Minirth, Frank B., and Meier, Paul D. *Happiness Is a Choice.* Grand Rapids, Mich.: Baker Book House, 1978.

Tournier, Paul. *Escape From Loneliness.* Philadelphia, Pa.: Westminster, 1976.

11

"I'm a Born Loser, Thanks to My Parents"
Defense Mechanisms and Self-esteem in Christ

Max was one of the sorriest people I had ever met. Nothing ever seemed to go right for him. He had barely managed to struggle through high school and had had a series of job failures since then. Recently he had been led to a saving knowledge of Jesus Christ, through the young-adults fellowship of the church he attended, and for the first time in his life, he went to his pastor to seek some counseling. His pastor quickly sent him to me.

"I'm a born loser, thanks to my parents," he began. "I'm a living example of Murphy's Law. If anything can go wrong in my life, it will!"

"Tell me about your parents and your upbringing," I encouraged him.

"Well, I'm an only child," he began, "so I had only school friends to play with when I was growing up, but I didn't have many of them. They all thought I was rather odd, not very outgoing, so I was pretty lonely. My father was an alcoholic, and my mother was a chronic schizophrenic. About every couple of years she'd quit taking her medicine, go crazy, and be in the hospital for a week or two.

"Neither of them showed me any love. I was never

hugged or kissed, except maybe when I was a baby, but I can't remember their ever giving me any affection. I got nothing but abuse and criticism. They were never happy with what I did, either at home or school. They didn't seem to really want me. Finally, when I was a teenager, my father died of cirrhosis of the liver, and my mother said she couldn't cope with me anymore. So I lived with her parents for about three years, but I went off on my own as soon as I finished high school."

"And what's happened since then?" I asked.

"Well, I couldn't get anything but manual labor, so I went into construction work, going from job to job, wherever I heard there was some building going on. Sometimes I got fired because I'd get so worried and wouldn't do a good enough job, but most of the time I got laid off when the job ended."

"What do you think you can do well? What helps you feel good about yourself?"

"I'm good at steel work, like welding. I learned it by doing it. I know something about steel scaffolding and girder construction. Usually I can get a job as a welder, but jobs are rare now, so I'm on unemployment again. Something should be opening up in a month or two, though."

"How do you feel about yourself as a person?" I asked.

"Pretty low, I guess," he replied. "I feel better when I'm employed. But otherwise I don't have a lot to do. My only friends are on the job, but they only last a few months, until the job is finished; then I usually never see them again."

"What about dating?"

"Before I was a Christian, I was interested in women for sex," Max told me. "But now I see them as equals. I respect them more, especially the ones I've met at church. I've dated one or two women from the fellowship, but I've got nothing to offer yet. If I had a regular job, I'd like to get married someday."

"How has becoming a Christian changed you?" I asked.

"Well, that's the biggest problem. That's why my pastor sent me to you. I was really excited when I first became a Christian, but now that's kind of worn off, and I find being a Christian very difficult. It is so different from the way I was brought up. I can't live up to the high moral standards people at my church expect. I've only stuck with it because they are so loving and accepting of me. They are my first true friends. Some of them are very beautiful people. It's hard, though, for me to identify with them."

"Would you like to identify with them?" I inquired.

"I guess so. They all seem to live a much more satisfying and fulfilling life than I do. I suppose I'd become a better person if I became more like some of them."

"*Identification* is a fairly simple mental mechanism," I said. "It is an unconscious process in which you model yourself upon the personality and characteristics of another person. In your case, you are very much the product of identification with your parents. Fortunately you can see that much of it was not good, since both your parents were not good role models. However, if you consciously allow yourself to continue in your church fellowship, you will find that gradually you will unconsciously begin to identify your personality and character structure with a few of them whom you especially admire and like.

"However remember that your ultimate objective in identification as a Christian will be with the person of Christ. Paul wrote to the Philippians, 'Let this mind be in you, which was also in Christ Jesus' [Philippians 2:5]. Christian growth consists largely of an ever-deepening identification with Jesus as personal Savior and Lord. The more He becomes the One to whom we look, the more we will grow to be like Him and be usable by Him to influence others. We should at all times be 'Looking unto Jesus the author and finisher of our faith. . .' [Hebrews 12:2]. Ultimately, of course, we will attain total identification, as John said, '. . .

when he shall appear, we shall be like him; for we shall see him as he is' " [1 John 3:2].

"What else can I do to live a fuller life?" Max asked.

"Fellowship with your Christian friends will naturally result from deeper fellowship with God, which in turn will lead to the fuller life. In order to attain this, it is essential that you be in a state of total repentance, so that you can receive total forgiveness. Remember that Christ died for all your sins: past, present, and future; remembered or forgotten; committed deliberately or in ignorance."

"I believe I'm forgiven," Max said, "but I keep remembering my former sins, and my feelings of guilt are spoiling my peace with God."

"Another mental mechanism that will help you, Max," I responded, "is *repression*. Like identification, this is sometimes called a defense mechanism and is also an unconscious process. It essentially amounts to forgetting. When God forgives, He also forgets, so we should do the same. '. . . For I will forgive their iniquity, and I will remember their sin no more' [Jeremiah 31:34]. A few hundred years earlier, King David wrote, 'As far as the east is from the west, so far hath he removed our transgressions from us' [Psalms 103:12].

"As Christians we need to bring up into conscious awareness all the sins we have committed earlier in life. Then once these are all confessed and repented, we are given by God the blessed assurance that every one of them is forever forgiven. Then we can forever forget them, by the healing process of repression, through which all painful or conflicting thoughts, impulses, or unpleasant memories are pushed down into the unconscious and excluded from the memory.

"When we are repentant and forgiven, God gives us the additional blessing of forgetting, so that the past no longer haunts us. In this way becoming a Christian enables one to start a new life. Old sins are forgotten because they are forgiven. We start afresh with a clean slate. Assurance of forgiveness gives the new Christian relief from the burden of sin and the freedom to begin a new life in Christ. Paul said, 'Therefore if any man be in Christ, he is a new creature: old things are passed away; behold, all things are become new' [2 Corinthians 5:17]."

"This is great," Max enthused, "but what do I do when some bad memories keep flashing back to me?"

"Another mental defense mechanism," I replied, "is *suppression.* This is the conscious equivalent of repression. In suppression, as soon as it is recognized, you deliberately put an unwanted thought out of your mind by replacing it with another pleasurable or interesting thought, which you dwell upon for several seconds.

"This exercise becomes more efficient with practice. The more often you do it, the less will your flash memories bother you, and eventually the less frequently will they appear. Above all keep remembering that all past sins are forgiven, and are therefore to be forgotten."

Max came back the following week, saying that he had both good news and bad news. The good news, he said, was that he had prayed with some of his new Christian friends and now felt a very refreshing new sense of being spiritually clean and forgiven for all his past sins. He said he was trying to forget the past and start living the new life. The bad news was that even though he felt forgiven for the past, he was still having problems in the present.

"It's this girl, Maria, at my church," he began, "she's the first girl I've dated who's a Christian, so I assumed she wouldn't want to have any sex with me, but to my surprise she was very physically responsive. We've told each other that we are in love, so we thought that therefore sex was okay. We didn't quite go all the way, but we really got pretty close. I guess I was waiting for her to put the brakes on, but eventually I had to. All she said was, 'Not the first time, please,' but we agreed it would be okay to go ahead next time, because we love each other."

"Max, you're talking about another psychological defense mechanism called *rationalization*. This is not the same as lying, which is a consciously produced deliberate falsehood intended to mislead another. Rationalization is deluding oneself by giving a generally socially acceptable and apparently logical explanation for an action motivated by repressed impulses that consciously you know to have been wrong. In your situation you have both let your profession of love for each other delude yourselves into believing that premarital fornication is okay. That certainly was your attitude before you were saved, but now you need to make up your mind as to whether or not you want to live as a Christian."

"Oh, I definitely do," affirmed Max. "And I'll try to wait until marriage before I have any more sex, but you know it's tough when you've gotten used to it!"

"I know, Max. I've been through it myself," I encouraged. "I was unmarried until I was thirty-seven, so I really empathize with you in your struggle. However remember that Jesus said, 'I am the . . . truth. . .' (John 14:6). Dwell on this thought. Pray about it. It will help you to live in the truth and stop deluding yourself."

He returned the following week, looking very dejected. "Still no job," he complained. "And Maria's become very unfriendly."

"What do you mean, 'unfriendly'?" I asked.

"She refuses to even let me hold her hand now, let alone kiss her or anything else. We had a bummer of a date last Saturday. She was so cold and unresponsive. She just gave me one-word answers. We had no conversation at all."

"Does she still profess to love you?" I asked.

"Well, yes, she says she does, but she sure didn't act like it last week," he complained.

"She's using a defense mechanism known as *undoing*," I said. "She feels guilty about your petting the previous week, so she's attempting to negate the effects and punish both of you for what you did. This cold aloofness reduces her guilt feelings and unconsciously undoes the damage caused to her Christian self-concept. All you need to do is to pray together and repent of your petting, and your good relationship will be restored."

"I'm not very good at praying out loud with anyone else," Max said, "but I'll give it a try."

The next week he was back with some new developments. "Good news and bad news, again," he started. "I may be getting a new job soon, but things are not working out with Maria. In fact I've starting dating someone else from the church. Her name is Ellen, and she's one of the leaders of the young adult group. She's a very mature Christian. I think she'd make a wonderful wife."

"Hmm . . . ," I replied. "Sounds a little too much like a rebound situation to me. Do you love her as you do Maria?"

"Well, quite honestly, no," he replied. "She really isn't my type, but she's a great Christian."

"Max," I said. "You're at it again. Now you're using two more mental mechanisms: *idealization* and *displacement.* You're idealizing Ellen by overestimating her good qualities, like her Christian maturity, but underestimating her undesirable qualities, mainly that she doesn't really appeal to you the way that Maria does. This is no fault of hers, but she's no good for you if you are merely attracted to her as an idealized Christian mate.

"Also, you've allowed your affections for Maria to be displaced to Ellen. You're justifying your change of love object by rationalizing that Ellen would make a better wife than Maria, simply because she's a more mature Christian. But if you don't love her, your displacement won't work out. You'd end up in divorce."

The following week Max was back with new problems. "I think I've got that job as a welder. There's some new building due to start next month. They'll let me know in a couple of weeks; but I had quite a scene with Ellen. I'd started to

cool it with her because of what you said last time about my
not really loving her, and she reacted most peculiarly."

"What happened?" I inquired.

"At our last fellowship meeting Ellen quite suddenly accused me in front of one or two others of making a pass at
her. I did nothing of the sort, and it was all very embarrassing!"

"You've brought this on yourself, Max," I said.

"First of all you manifested what is known as *reaction
formation* towards Ellen. Realizing that she was not a suit-
able mate for you, you suddenly started acting cold toward
her. This was an overcompensation for your unwanted initial feelings of attraction toward her, in which you went to
the opposite extreme. You reacted to your realization that
you had made a mistake by forming an aloof attitude towards her.

"Ellen then reacted with what is known as *projection.* You
had aroused sexual feelings within her, and she became dis-
tressed when you reversed yourself and acted coldly toward
her. Her accusation was a projection onto you of her own
sexual feelings, which she was trying to deny as a defense
against your rejection of her. Projection is potentially dan-
gerous. It represents a denial of truth and can lead to paranoid delusions of persecution, which in turn could result in
violent defense reactions against innocent people."

"Boy, I sure seem to be in a mess," Max groaned. "Maybe
I should just curl up and hide somewhere."

"No, Max, that's not necessary," I reassured him. "Just
have a straight talk with Ellen and explain that you love her
as a sister in Christ, but that you made a mistake in saying
what you did to give her wrong ideas about you. If she's as
mature as you say she is, she'll understand and forgive you."

Max came again to announce that his new job was to start
in two weeks and that he and Maria were going together
again. He was having a problem, however, convincing her
that he would be a good husband.

"What's the problem?" I asked.

"Well, we've reasserted our love for each other," he began, "but she's apprehensive about my job history. I've tried to reassure her, but she wants to wait until I've proved myself as far as a stable income is concerned before she'll make any commitment."

"And how have you reacted to that?" I questioned. He looked down to the floor and seemed to be somewhat embarrassed and ashamed.

"I guess I've tried to prove myself as a man," he confessed. "So we've gotten more involved sexually again. She seems to be pretty happy with me in that area, though we both feel guilty."

"Max," I said. "This is known as *compensation*. You are understandably concerned about your income prospects, so you have compensated by convincing Maria of your masculinity by extending your physical relationship. This is unlikely to reduce your sense of inadequacy in the financial area, though that will almost certainly improve with time; in any case, having sex is not the ultimate answer. You don't need to prove yourself in this area. By the way, are you and Maria using any birth-control methods?"

"Well, er—no." Max admitted. "I guess we thought it would be a sin to buy them."

"A greater sin than her getting pregnant?" I needled.

"No, I suppose not. We just hoped she wouldn't get pregnant. We didn't actually quite go that far," he stammered.

"Max, this is *denial*. Either you and Maria are both denying the reality of the possibility of pregnancy, or you have an unspoken assumption that you will get married or have an abortion if she does. You are failing to recognize and admit to the possible consequences of your actions. You are both unconsciously rejecting the intolerable thought of pregnancy by a protective nonawareness."

"I don't know what all that means," Max complained, "but neither of us agrees with abortion. I suppose if she gets pregnant we'd either get married or give the baby up for adoption. But I'm praying it won't come to that."

"So what do you plan to do about it?" I pressed him.

"I guess I'll ask her to marry me and trust the Lord about my employment situation."

"And sex?" I asked.

"I'll try not to have sex with her again until we're married, but it's going to be difficult."

"Of course," I said, "but there's one final mental defense mechanism you can use to help you during the waiting period. It's called *sublimation*."

"What's that?" Max asked.

"Sublimation is a means of reducing the effects of an uncontrollable drive, such as the need for sex, by diverting those energies into more socially acceptable activities. For example, the energies of your sexual drive can be diverted into creative activities such as hobbies, artistic pursuits, religion, or physical exercise and competitive sports. Also once you become employed again, striving to become really first class at your job and maybe trying to advance yourself within your firm will also divert some of your pent-up energies."

"I guess I could do most of what you suggest," Max said. "I enjoy listening to music; I take my religion seriously; and I can get back to jogging again. These should effect what you suggest, but they can at best be only temporary. Eventually of course, Maria and I will probably get married once I'm settled in my job."

"That's good, Max," I said. "I'm confident that things will work out for you both, but now let me just weigh a couple of things about your sense of self-esteem.

"Admittedly you've had a pretty rough start in life, but having gotten to know you, I'm satisfied that you've got what it takes, both in intelligence and personality, to be successful. Your parents never gave you a high sense of self-worth, so you entered the adult world feeling like a failure to start with. Your low self-confidence level made you feel anxious, and your anxiety led to actual inadequacy, so you got yourself into a no-win vicious circle of job failure. You need to forgive your parents for their poor upbringing of you and strive to rise above the deprivations they inflicted on you.

"All this is possible for you, especially now that you are a believer. You must forgive and forget the past, evaluate your abilities in the present, and live for the future. God has given you a skill, a good job starting soon, and a fine Christian girl as your future wife.

"Read Jesus' parables of the talents and the pounds in Matthew twenty-five, verses fourteen through thirty, and Luke nineteen, verses twelve through twenty-seven. Remember also that Jesus said, '. . . unto whomsoever much is given, of him shall be much required. . .' [Luke 12:48]. You've had a bad background and therefore a slow start in life, but you are nevertheless in the 'much given, much required' category.

"You're intelligent, skilled in your job, physically and mentally healthy, and have motivation and enthusiasm. Also God has given you a strong and attractive personality; a bride; good employment; and best of all, a knowledge of Himself, with the assurance of salvation and security through this life that comes with it. Remember also that Paul describes us who are believers as ". . . heirs of God, and joint-heirs with Christ. . .' [Romans 8:17]. Peter says that we are destined 'To an inheritance incorruptible, and undefiled, and that fadeth not away, reserved in heaven for you' [1 Peter 1:4]. These facts should help you feel pretty good about yourself!"

"Wow! You make me sound like a winner!" Max exclaimed.

"Exactly, Max," I encouraged. "You've got what it takes to be a winner. Developing a good self-image and a sense of self-confidence—which you can do if you stick with it—will lead to feelings of acceptance, belonging, self-worth, and the ability to love yourself."

"Love myself?" he queried.

"Yes. Jesus said, '. . . Love thy neighbour as thyself. . .' [Mark 12:31]. To love yourself is to have a good sense of self-esteem. When you've developed this—which you are now in the process of doing—you will find that you will be able to love your neighbor as yourself, and this will lead to greatly improved relationships with other people both socially and on the job. Nothing succeeds like success, and you and Maria are headed that way!"

Max's new job turned out to be a lot better than he had thought, and a year later he was made a foreman. Shortly afterwards, he and Maria married, and he wrote later saying they were soon to have their first child. In his letter he thanked me for helping him to understand himself and for encouraging him in the personal, vocational, and spiritual aspects of his life, all of which he said were now going very well.

Questions

1. Do you have a good sense of self-esteem? If so, upon what (or whom) is it based? What memories make you feel down about yourself? What memories make you feel good about yourself? Share these in your group and react to the memories and feelings of others.

2. Look through the several psychological mechanisms summarized in this chapter. Which ones are "good" or at least helpful? Which ones are "bad" or self-destructive? Which ones could be either, depending on circumstances?

3. Share examples with your group of ways in which you have become aware of using some of these mechanisms.

Have some been a means of avoiding responsibility? Have some been used to help you in a difficult situation? Could you have used one or two of them to protect the feelings of others? Discuss your consciously realized motivations in using these often unconscious mechanisms for whatever purposes.

4. Look through the several verses of Scripture quoted in this chapter. Pray and think about them by yourself and ask the Holy Spirit to apply them to your own life. Then discuss them with others: Philippians 2:5; Hebrews 12:2; Jeremiah 31:34; Psalms 103:12; 2 Corinthians 5:17; John 14:6; Matthew 25:14–30; Luke 19:12–27; Luke 12:48; Romans 8:17; 1 Peter 1:4; Mark 12:31.

For Further Study

Augsburger, David. *Caring Enough to Confront.* Rev. ed. Glendale, Calif.: Regal, 1980.

Birkey, Verna. *You Are Very Special.* Old Tappan, N.J.: Fleming H. Revell, 1977.

Dobson, James. *Hide or Seek.* Old Tappan, N.J.: Fleming H. Revell, 1974.

Ginott, Haim. *Between Parent and Child.* New York: Avon, 1969.

Narramore, Bruce. *You're Someone Special.* 2nd ed. Grand Rapids, Mich.: Zondervan, 1980.

Osborne, Cecil. *The Art of Learning to Love Yourself.* Grand Rapids, Mich.; Zondervan, 1976.

Powell, John. *Why Am I Afraid to Tell You Who I Am?* Allen, Tex.: Argus, 1969.

Schmidt, Paul F. *Coping With Difficult People.* Philadelphia, Pa.: Westminster, 1980.

Tournier, Paul. *The Meaning of Persons.* New York: Harper & Row, 1957.

Wagner, Maurice. *Put It All Together: Developing Inner Security.* Grand Rapids, Mich.: Zondervan, 1978.

12

"We've Got a Terrible Marriage"

Priorities and Communication

How can one describe a typical or average marriage? People are so different—and therefore their marriages are, too—that it would be difficult. But Sean and Allison's had many factors in common with the majority of the middle-aged couples I've counseled over twenty years.

"We've got a terrible marriage," Allison started, "and it's getting worse. We just don't seem to communicate anymore, and we can't agree on priorities. Sean is so selfish: He always wants his own way, always puts himself first, even before the kids. We seem to have drifted apart in the twenty-five years we've been married. He's got his golf every weekend and his city club weeknights. He's only occasionally home for supper with the family. Whenever he comes with me to any local community function, he's always so bored it's embarrassing."

"What's the problem as you see it?" I asked turning to Sean.

"She's a spendthrift," Sean replied, "constantly buying things for the house, most of which we don't need. She thinks I'm made of money. Also I'm sick and tired of her nagging. I can't do anything right; she's always criticizing me or my friends or my social life. She's become very frigid recently, too. She not only doesn't seem to enjoy lovemaking anymore, she has started to refuse me altogether. Our sex life has been a total bust in the last several months."

"What's happening spiritually?" I inquired.

"That's another thing," Allison added. "Sean used to be an elder in our church, even taught the adult Sunday-school Bible class for a year or so. Now he's not even the spiritual leader in our home. He says a perfunctory prayer before meals, when he graces us with his presence, but it's been months since we had a family altar together."

"The kids are turned off," Sean added. "They won't come to church with us anymore and say we are hypocrites. They seemed to enjoy Sunday school when they were younger, but now they have no interest even in the young people's fellowship, let alone the worship service."

In order to find out the story more fully, I told Sean and Allison that I would have to see both of them two or three times each individually and that then, once I had fairly well understood their situation from both points of view, I would begin seeing them as a couple and work with them toward improving communication and establishing agreed-upon priorities. It was arranged that I would see Sean weekly in my Manhattan office on his way home in the early evening, and Allison would see me in my suburban office on a weekday in the mid-morning.

Sean came first, and he described or exhibited several of the classical symptoms of marital breakdown.

"What's the use?" he started despairingly. "I think it's probably already too late. I'm not even sure if I care anymore. She's always attacking me both openly and privately, always criticizing my appearance, achievements, even my sexuality. I can't win. My best intentions or efforts she shoots down. Sometimes I think I just want out so that I can start a new life. Whenever we try to discuss our difficulties, I just get an endless repetition of old issues and arguments that never get resolved. Sometimes I'm tempted to think that if I ignore our problems they'll just go away. I guess I tend to deny or avoid them, but rationally I know we have to face the issues and deal with them."

Allison was even more dejected about their situation when I saw her.

"It's a complete communication breakdown," she started. "We're not on the same wavelength at all. He's so withdrawn, wanting to be left alone, doing his own thing. I've had it. There's no hope for us. Is it my fault or his—or both of us? What's gone wrong? I'm so confused I don't know what to do. You are our last hope. If you can't help us, we'll have to get ourselves lawyers and arrange a separation."

I saw them alone three or four more times each and then arranged a session with them together, feeling that I could begin to see their situation from both points of view.

"You're both right about communication breakdown," I started. "It's at the root of your problems. However I don't believe it's too late, on condition that you are both motivated to give your marriage one last try. You've got twenty-five years of your lives invested in your relationship and four teenage and young-adult children you have to finish raising and educating. If you're both willing to make some changes, even sacrifices, I believe I can help; but if either of you wants to quit, I can't help. You've both got to want it."

They nodded their acquiescence less than enthusiastically, but neither wanted to back out. Both had said to me individually that they each could possibly rekindle love for the other, if certain minimum changes were made. I shared with both of them what those changes were and helped them start the process of arriving at some mutually acceptable compromise.

"Sean, the main change on your part needs to be a realignment of your priorities. I'm not going to order you to make changes, because you'd only resist if I did. I'm merely going to make suggestions and ask questions on the basis of my understanding and integration of what you and Allison have told me over the last two or three weeks.

"First, with regard to time, take your daily and weekly schedule. How can these be changed to demonstrate to Allison and the children that you really do have their best interests at heart? I don't need an answer from you now. I just ask you to think about some sacrifices you might be willing to make in the area of your social and sporting pleasures in order to spend more time at home with them.

"Second, please realize that you and Allison are only going to be reunited as a happy couple on a permanent basis if you develop activities in common. For example, if you could be more interested in her volunteer community work, involving yourself in occasional evening meetings with people who are strangers to you, maybe she would be willing to take an interest in some of the things you do. For example, she could take up golf, and with the handicap system would soon be able to play with you competitively, which would be a lot of fun."

"I'd like that," Sean said. "Lots of my friends play with their wives on Saturday afternoons. It would be enjoyable to join them next season." Allison looked at him with an "I can't believe my ears" look on her face.

"Good. Now, third. I sympathise with your wanting to spend time with your buddies at your midtown club," I said, smiling, "but wouldn't once weekly be sufficient? Couldn't you come home in time for supper on other weekday evenings? Even if not for Allison, your children would like to see more of you on a daily basis.

"Finally I strongly urge you to reassert your spiritual leadership in the home. You'll have to win back the children on this one, but they need your guidance and knowledge of the deep things of God that you formerly pursued. They are at a very crucial age right now, especially the younger ones. The biblical instruction you could give them and the example of a good private and family prayer life you will show and teach them could inspire them to Christian maturity themselves and train them to become leaders also in their own future homes and churches, when they have grown up, married, and left home."

He didn't deny or challenge anything I said, only asked a few questions for amplification of some points.

I turned to Allison and said, "Allison, Sean obviously has some valid complaints, too. Again I'm not ordering you to make changes; I'm asking you to consider some modifications to your daily and weekly routine. He's got a good point about your shopping sprees. You've admitted yourself that several things you buy you find you don't have as much use for as you thought you would. In today's economy, we all need to tighten our belts a little. You're already living at a reasonably high socioeconomic level. You've already got all you need. Anything else is either unnecessary or just pure luxury.

"Consider also the matter of nagging. I admit that you've got a lot to nag about, but you must have seen how it only leads to Sean's angry retreat. He not only doesn't respond and do what you want, but he further withdraws.

"With regard to your sex life," I continued, "I think it may be too early in the process of healing to reactivate that, but maybe not. I suggest you first talk with each other about the issues we've talked about today and see if you can come to some measure of agreement. Since the motivation to heal your marriage seems to have increased in the past month, you might soon be ready to return to your sexual relationship. Don't push it. See how you both feel toward each other and let your physical responsiveness develop spontaneously."

They left, and as recommended they had a surprisingly friendly conversation alone together over the weekend. Both were scared of divorce: the potential loneliness, the financial burden, the public shame, and the effect on the children. They decided it was worth giving their marriage one last try.

The following week they returned together, minimally optimistic that things could work out.

"We've both agreed to make changes," Allison started. "Sean has promised to be home for supper at least five evenings every week and to come with me and be friendly at our community meetings. I've promised to cut down on my bargain shopping and not to buy anything expensive unless we both agree that either the house or one of the kids really needs it."

"What about the nagging?" I asked Sean.

"Well, she's been pretty good this past week," Sean said. "Almost like when we were first married. We think we're communicating better, but we'd like some feedback and advice from you."

"Okay," I said. "Since you're obviously both beginning to move back toward each other, perhaps you are now ready to listen. Let me say a few things about priorities and communication.

"The Christian's first priority should be God and his relationship with Him. Next comes his wife (or husband, for a woman), then his children, his job, his church, his other social obligations, and finally himself—in that order, which I submit is biblical. Any divergence from this hierarchy of priorities can adversely affect inner peace and contentment in the Christian life. Church is low on the list in the sense of an organization in which a man or woman might have responsibilities. If God is your top priority, you will be guided in accordance with His will with regard to all the others.

"Good communication results from a mutual understanding of both meanings and feelings—of both verbal and nonverbal exchanges. The purpose of good communication is to produce meaningful action or change. Nonverbal communication can be very significant and meaningful. Actions spead louder than words, as the cliché goes. The 'silent treatment' can be a very effective way of getting a message across. Thousands of elderly couples in our country live out their declining years in a state of lonely, silent hostility.

"But that is all negative. I mention it with the prayer that you will avoid it. The positive side of nonverbal communication is the changes you have said you are willing to make. If Sean in fact comes home evenings, stops being so selfish, and is more friendly at local meetings, he will be nonverbally communicating his willingness to restore your marital accord. Similarly, if Allison in fact controls her excessive spending and stops nagging, these actions will speak louder than any words she could speak."

"Sometimes I feel Sean just isn't listening to me," Allison complained.

"Speech is only one part of good communication," I replied, addressing both of them. "A second part is hearing with understanding, and a third part is responding, whether by agreeing or disagreeing. For example, if while Allison is talking, Sean, you are already thinking of what you are going to say in response, you are not really hearing or understanding her. You therefore cannot respond appropriately, because you have prevented yourself from sincerely attempting to understand her point of view. This way you can never expect to arrive at an agreeable compromise. You both need to understand thoroughly the other's point of view on any issue before you can possibly come to an agreement."

"I follow you," said Sean, "and I admit I've been guilty of not listening. I guess her constant nagging switched off my ability to hear her. But she's better now; so I'll try harder. Any other suggestions?"

"Just one more thing for today," I replied. "Try to arrange your schedules so that you can get away alone together, away from the children, on a fairly regular basis. My wife and I have sustained good communication throughout our marriage by spending one evening every week and one full weekend every three months alone together away from our three children.

"You both seem to be moving in the right direction, so stick with it. Next week I want to share some well known verses of Scripture with you, which I hope will seal permanently your newfound desire to make your marriage a happy one."

Progress continued, though slowly at first, between Allison and Sean. Sean reasserted his spiritual leadership in the home, and Allison gradually became more responsive affectionally and eventually sexually. When they came to see me for the last time, I handed them each a Bible to look at with me for a few minutes, and asked them to turn to 1 Corinthians 13:4–7.

"Let us in conclusion go through God's description of love as given to us by the apostle Paul. Start first at verse four. We'll go phrase by phrase."

" 'Love suffereth long.' This means to be patient, not quickly angry or irritated, and accepting of the personality, temperament, and unique characteristics of each other. It encompasses mutual submission one to the other.

" 'And is kind.' Love realizes the other person's needs and strives to meet them as fully as it is within your power to do so. To be kind is to be tender, compassionate, gentle, and caring.

" 'Love envieth not.' Be content with all that God has given you in gifts, talents, abilities, opportunities, and friends, of whom your best is your spouse. Envy is different from jealousy. Envy is wanting something someone else has. Jealousy is wishing they didn't have it. '. . . I the Lord thy God am a jealous God . . .' [Exodus 20:5], wanting Israel not to have other gods. It is not appropriate for a Christian woman to be envious of the possessions or qualities of another woman. It *is* appropriate for her to be jealous if the other woman is her husband's mistress.

" 'Love vaunteth not itself.' Don't try to impress others or create a possibly false image for personal benefit.

" 'Is not puffed up.' Be humble toward each other. Control the temptation to have inflated ideas about yourself. We must not be self-centered or so full of our own importance that we expect the earth to revolve around us.

" 'Doth not behave itself unseemly.' Have respect and good manners toward each other. Be discreet, proper, and have Christ-centered standards in relating to one another.

" 'Seeketh not her own.' Don't let the satisfaction of your own needs and appetites take precedence over meeting those of your spouse. Put his or her need above your own in all decisions.

" 'Is not easily provoked.' Don't overreact in any disagreement. In rejecting an idea, don't reject the person with the idea. Don't be overly sensitive, easily hurt or touchy, or take things too personally. At all times try to see both sides of an argument.

" 'Thinketh no evil.' Subdue suspiciousness. Think good, not evil of your spouse. Don't keep a list of wrongs. Don't drag up the past. Never resurrect an old hurt that has been forgiven. Forgive and forget. Live for the future, not the past.

" 'Rejoiceth not in iniquity.' Avoid the temptation to enjoy vicarious pleasure from the sins of others or to compare yourself favorably with others' personal weaknesses. Never attempt to justify sin on the basis that 'everybody does it.'

" 'But rejoiceth in the truth.' Not only tell the truth, but live the truth. 'Do that which is right in the sight of the Lord.' Consider it a compliment if someone calls you a 'straight arrow.' You're convicting him of the untruths and inconsistencies in his life.

" 'Beareth all things.' This means that in a loving relationship there is no limit to your forebearance one for the other. You learn to live with the other's faults and truly empathize with him or her in all personal problems.

" 'Believeth all things.' You believe in each other and trust each other fully. You have a high regard for your spouse's worth and integrity.

" 'Hopeth all things.' This is confidence that the same God who brought you together in the past in love will keep you together in the future and, so long as you desire it, will enable your mutual love for each other to grow.

" 'Endureth all things.' God can give to both of you the ability to endure in your love even in the face of all obstacles, disappointments, and even unreturned love from the other. God will enable you to remain faithful to Himself and to each other, until He calls you by death to be forever in His presence."

Questions

Note: *This chapter should preferably be discussed in mixed groups, so that both male and female viewpoints can be shared.*

1. Discuss as openly as possible the different complaints that Sean and Allison had about each other. Add your own personal experiences, either similar or different, which have adversely affected your own marital harmony. What have you and your spouse done so far to improve the situation?

2. Think and pray about priorities in your life as a marital partner and as a parent. Do you have an agreed hierarchy of priorities with your spouse? If not, talk and pray together about one.

3. How do you and your spouse communicate? Are you both "up front" and honest? Or do you both give or receive the "silent treatment"? What in your experience has or could cause communication breakdown? What have you done or could you do to improve marital communication?

4. Spend time in a mixed group thoroughly discussing 1 Corinthians 13:4–7, specifically applying all the points to the marital relationship.

For Further Study

Augsburger, David. *Caring Enough to Forgive.* Ventura, Calif.: Regal, 1981.

Clinebell, Howard J., and Clinebell, Charlotte H. *The Intimate Marriage.* New York: Harper & Row, 1970.

Cooper, Darien B. *You Can Be the Wife of a Happy Husband.* Wheaton, Ill.: Victor, 1974.

Dobson, James. *What Wives Wish Their Husbands Knew About Women.* Wheaton, Ill.: Tyndale, 1975.

Evans, Louis. *Your Marriage—Duel or Duet.* Old Tappan, N.J.: Fleming H. Revell, 1972.

LaHaye, Tim. *How to Be Happy Though Married.* Wheaton, Ill.: Tyndale, 1968.

Masters, William H. et al. *The Pleasure Bond.* New York: Bantam, 1976.

Powell, John. *The Secret of Staying in Love.* Allen, Tex.: Argus, 1974.

Smoke, Jim. *Growing Through Divorce.* Eugene, Ore.: Harvest House, 1979.

Swindoll, Charles R. *Strike the Original Match.* Portland, Ore.: Multnomah, 1980.

Vayhinger, John. *Before Divorce.* Edited by William E. Hulme. Philadelphia, Pa.: Fortress, 1972.

Wheat, Ed, and Wheat, Gaye. *Intended for Pleasure.* Rev. ed. Old Tappan, N.J.: Fleming H. Revell, 1981.

Wright, H. Norman. *Communication: Key to Your Marriage.* Ventura, Calif.: Regal, 1979.

13

"Oh, My Many Aches and Pains!"
Physical Effects of Mental Anguish

In the third millenium B.C., Huang Ti, the Yellow Emperor of China, wrote that anxiety can cause changes in the body as well as the mind. Hippocrates (460–377 B.C.) first recognised that the brain was the distribution center for feelings and intelligence and commented on the relationship between emotional arousal and an asthmatic attack. Henry Maudsley, a famous English nineteenth-century physician said, "The sorrow which has no vent in tears may make other organs weep."

This is not hard to understand. The production of tears by the lacrimal glands, in the outer corner of the eyes, is clearly a physical effect that can be brought on by a purely emotional experience such as seeing a sad movie or experiencing an acute personal loss or disappointment. Suppose, however, that for some reason the emotion cannot be adequately expressed by simply crying. Other organs can be affected, especially if the cause is of long duration.

Your physical body acts as a mediator between yourself as a psychological entity (soul and spirit) and your external environment. It is your personal organ of communication. These upsets may be expressed: symbolically, as in a hysterical conversion reaction; through physical symptoms without actual disease; through real organic illness; through hypochondriac, excessive preoccupation with bodily functions; or through actual body-image changes, such as obesity.

Jane was a sixteen-year-old girl who had had a terrible argument with her father because she had come home late one night from a date, without calling home. As a punishment her father forbade her to stay out late again for a month. Her immediate desire was to clench her fist and punch her father in the face, but she just managed to control herself. After her rage had subsided, she began to feel guilty and somewhat frightened of her impulse to have struck him. The following morning she awoke to find her right hand paralyzed, but seemed to show no concern about it.

The essential dynamics of this situation is that Jane had unconsciously converted her internal conflict and anxiety to the physical symptom of paralyzing the hand that would have hit her father. Symbolically this represented to her admission of guilt and acted as a form of self-punishment. For her that was easier to live with than the internal anxiety and guilt feelings, and it represented for her what is known as primary gain. In addition she obtained a secondary gain in the form of increased attention, concern, and sympathy from her parents.

Hysterical conversion reactions, like Jane's, most often occur in neurotic personalities who are emotionally unstable, egocentric, sexually provocative, and who have strong dependency needs and hostile feelings. Lack of affection from parents early in life leads to this type of immature, dependent personality. When these facts were pointed out to Jane and her parents, her paralysis disappeared, and a much more mature family relationship between them all resulted.

The commonest psychosomatic conditions are those in which a patient complains of a variety of physical symptoms without any real organic disease. These are usually very destructive to the doctor-patient relationship. The patient is angry at the doctor, because he tells him he is physically okay, and often any symptomatic treatment is a failure. The doctor is angry at the patient, because he has no sooner treated one symptom than another one appears.

Common symptoms include headaches, insomnia, backaches, heart palpitations, hyperventilation, increased urinary frequency, menstrual disorders, impotence, frigidity, diarrhea, constipation, stomachache, nausea, indigestion, and a wide variety of vague, transient aches and pains that can affect any part of the whole body. From this abbreviated list, you can see why it is estimated that almost half of all patients seen initially by a family physician have complaints that are of emotional origin, not a physical one.

Sometimes real, demonstrable disease, with actual anatomical changes, can develop from emotional origins. Commonest among these are gastric ulcers, ulcerative colitis, high blood pressure, angina (heart pain), migraine, asthma, arthritis, obesity, some endocrine-gland abnormalities, and a variety of skin diseases.

Personality types often tend to predispose particular psychosomatic ailments. For example, the Type-A personality is the hard-driving, overworked, success-oriented businessman, who, especially if he smokes and takes no exercise, is very vulnerable to angina attacks and even a coronary thrombosis. The man with pent-up hostility, aggressive impulses, and uptight tension anxiety tends to develop high blood pressure.

Sufferers from asthma tend to be anxious, easily irritated, submissive, lacking in self-confidence, and dependent. Colitis is found in the very anxious person who has unconscious resentments, anger, guilt feelings, and feelings of insecurity and low self-esteem. Migraine occurs most often in high-strung, ambitious, perfectionistic people with rigid conventions and high standards and demands. Although arthritis is an inherited condition, its earliest symptoms and later acute attacks are almost always related to a period of emotional stress.

Bob came to see me several months ago, referred by his family doctor, who had been treating him for a gastric ulcer.

"Dr. Stewart says that my ulcer will never heal unless I get psychiatric treatment," said Bob. "I don't consider myself to be a head case, but he said you can help me even though I'm not crazy! He agrees that I'm not 'nuts,' but feels I've got a lot of problems in my life, which are preventing my ulcer from healing."

"What are the sorts of problems he thinks are affecting you?" I inquired.

"Well, I'm very active and work hard—nothing wrong with that—but Dr. Stewart says I'm too easily upset and get frustrated quickly when things go wrong. I'm very impatient, and every day I seem to be tense, nervous, uptight, or on edge most of the time. He says I'm too competitive, hard-driving, aggressive, determined, and that I put myself under too much pressure to achieve success. It's made me anxious, worried, overworked, and under constant emotional strain. He says I also suffer from guilt, insecurity, and have a strong desire to prove myself."

"What a classic description!" I exclaimed. "You could write a textbook account of the personality structure and life-style of a typical ulcer patient."

He told me about his background: a self-made man from a poor family, who had grown up determined to give his children what he had lacked as a child and to attain the financial success that had always eluded his father.

Psychotherapy consisted of talking through the various stressors in his life, one by one, and of how they could all be eliminated or at least reduced. In addition to reducing his stress, we needed to talk about his underlying attitudes. He needed to realize that he could continue his career effectively without such heavy self-imposed pressures.

I also explained to him the probable mechanism that had initially caused his ulcer and then perpetuated it, thereby frustrating medical treatment. The emotional center in a part of the brain called the *hypothalamus,* when stimulated by anger or anxiety, itself stimulates the adrenal glands, located near the kidneys, to produce more adrenaline and also makes the gastric juices more acidic.

The increased adrenaline decreases blood flow to the stomach wall, reducing its ability to resist the eroding action of the acid. This destroys the cells of the mucous membrane, the inner lining of the stomach, causing gastritis, with its symptoms of nausea, indigestion, stomachache and heartburn, or acid regurgitation. The gastritis, if not treated early, becomes an ulcer, as the acid literally eats its way through the stomach wall. A complete perforation through the wall can cause death by internal infection or hemorrhage.

Initial treatment is primarily medical, the high acidity being reduced by taking over-the-counter alkalis or other antacids. Surgical removal of the ulcer is needed if these fail, but another will recur on another part of the stomach wall unless the causes of the problem are dealt with. Bob was fortunate that combined medical and psychiatric treatment eventually healed his ulcer without the need for an operation.

In addition to psychotherapy aimed at reducing his stressful life-style, Bob and I talked about the way a spiritual experience could significantly modify his self-destructive personality structure. He came eventually to the point of yielding his life, with all its ambitions, under the Lordship of Christ. As he grew as a Christian he found an ever-increasing serenity, inner peace, ability to relax, and a proper sense of priorities in his work and homelife.

Another manifestation of the influence of the mind on the body is the condition known as *hypochondriasis,* which is a persistent overconcern with bodily health. This condition usually starts with some real but minor physical problems such as a common cold, a headache, a few nights of insomnia, or some indigestion or diarrhea. After recovery, the patient discovers other minor problems in different and often widely separated parts of the body. This leads to a preoccupation with the functioning of many bodily organs.

Common symptoms of the hypochondriacal person include such vague complaints as poor memory, inability to concentrate, pressure in the head, irritability, insomnia, and multiple transient aches and pains in any part of the body. The sufferer will describe these compulsively and repeatedly, to the point of great frustration and impatience on the part of the victimized listener, whether he or she is a sympathetic relative, friend, neighbor, pastor, or physician.

Frequently this problem is the patient's way of compensating for serious defects in self-esteem or for failures in life, or it is a method of diverting and limiting diffuse emotional pain into a localized physical one. The wide variety of complaints the hypochondriac describes can even lead to major surgery or therapeutic treatment that brings only temporary relief, if any at all. The secondary gains of increased sympathy and attention appeal to the insecure person who has feelings of low self-worth.

Only when the patient can be brought to realize that his body is in fact healthy and that his complaints represent unfulfilled emotional needs can psychiatric treatment be effective. Strong directive therapy from a doctor he trusts can sometimes inspire the patient to conquer negative feelings and return to responsible functioning. Group therapy with other hypochondriacs can help by allowing them all to share their various complaints.

I have found Paul's assertion to Timothy to be helpful for the Christian hypochondriac. "For God hath not given us the spirit of fear; but of power, and of love, and of a sound [responsible] mind" (2 Timothy 1:7).

A final situation in which the mind and body interact abnormally is body-image changes. This may occur after the amputation of a breast for cancer or of a lower leg for gangrene; but by far the commonest, usually unwanted, change is the development of obesity.

Obesity itself is not as detrimental to one's health as the factors causing it: a diet high in fats and sugars and a lifestyle of inadequate physical exercise (*see* chapter fourteen). Sometimes certain metabolic disorders or a hormone imbalance, which may be treated medically, also cause obesity. But in most cases, emotional deprivation, depression, or low self-esteem has led to eating as a substitute for love or appreciation. For a few sad persons, eating is the only pleasure in life they regularly look forward to. An excess of this dimension leads to gluttony, which is inescapably punished by undesirable weight gain and a potentially shortened life span.

Fad diets and appetite-suppressant medications usually provide only temporary results. The best solution is to develop the habit of eating nutritionally good food in lesser quantities and combining it with a gradually escalating exercise program (*see* chapter fourteen). The support of a group of fellow sufferers, a technique used by Overeaters Anonymous or Weight Watchers groups, may also help.

Although I doubt the writer to the Hebrews had gluttony in mind, these words are appropriate for most psychosomatic patients: ". . . Let us lay aside every weight, and the sin which doth so easily beset us, and let us run with patience the race that is set before us, Looking unto Jesus the author and finisher of our faith . . ." (Hebrews 12:1, 2).

Questions

1. Share personal examples of how emotional upsets of any kind have produced physical effects, in your experience. Do you agree that "the sorrow which has no vent in tears

may make other organs weep"? Can you give any examples in yourself or others known to you?

2. Discuss the five types of psychosomatic manifestations outlined in this chapter. In what ways are they similar? In what ways different?

3. Think and talk about the widespread problem of moderate overweight or even gross obesity in this country. Why do you think most American adults eat too much?

4. What should this nation do about our deplorable waste of food caused by overproduction or discarding of surplus supplies or leftovers by hotels, restaurants, and private homes? Discuss why we die young from the effects of overeating, while millions elsewhere in the world die young from undernutrition. How can we move toward a moral solution to this problem? What about those starving in our own country?

5. Think, pray about and discuss the two verses quoted in this chapter: 2 Timothy 1:7; Hebrews 12:1, 2.

For Further Study

Cheraskin, E. *Psychodietetics.* New York: Bantam, 1976.

Havner, Vance. *Though I Walk Through the Valley.* Old Tappan, N.J.: Fleming H. Revell, 1974.

Larson, Bruce. *There's a Lot More to Health Than Not Being Sick.* Waco, Tex.: Word Books, 1981.

McMillen, S. I. *None of These Diseases.* Old Tappan, N.J.: Fleming H. Revell, 1963.

Tournier, Paul. *Learn to Grow Old.* New York: Harper & Row, 1973.

Yancey, Philip. *Where Is God When It Hurts.* Grand Rapids, Mich.: Zondervan, 1977.

14

"I'm So Unfit and Overweight!"
Principles of Diet and Exercise

Recently I went to a gathering of friends in the home of a local Christian leader. During the course of conversation, our host expounded on the evils of alcohol and told how he and his wife had never had a drop of the "wicked poison" in their house in all the years they had been married. None of us disagreed with their principles; some expressed admiration for their uprightness and self-discipline. However, I could not help but observe that both were grossly overweight. They had lived purely as far as liquor was concerned, but they had spent their time indulging in gluttony!

What one *does* speaks louder than what one *says*. Our host was within his rights both in abstaining from alcohol and in testifying to its evils, but he was not living a truly disciplined Christian life. His indulgence in food was not only just as physically harmful to his body as alcohol, but it also canceled out what he said about the principles of Christian discipline.

Gluttony and its inevitable consequences, obesity, are probably Christianity's most acceptable sins. Historically this emerged in the Dark Ages, when monks, nuns, and priests made threefold vows of poverty, chastity, and obedience. What was left for them to do that gave physical pleasure? Eating and drinking. Fat old Friar Tuck is for many the image of a medieval monk. Those who dedicated themselves to the church could not afford other worldly pleasures; their vows forbade marriage and even spending money on themselves, and the semimilitary discipline of their daily routine was extremely rigorous.

As a result, the church has continued to condone gluttony as a "minor" sin. In terms of its potential harm to the body, the Christian's temple of the Holy Spirit, food in excess of exercise expenditure is far from a minor sin. Overeating becomes culpably self-destructive.

Christians need to be informed about how to combat this temptation. They must learn to reduce their dietary intake and must increase their caloric expenditure, through physical exercise, to control weight by burning up any excesses taken in.

Long ago a friend of mine quoted Mark Twain: "Whenever I feel the urge to take some exercise, I sit down until the urge passes off!" He died grossly overweight, at not even fifty years of age, of a sudden, acute heart attack. Paul said: ". . . Whatsoever a man soweth, that shall he also reap: For he that soweth to his flesh shall of the flesh reap corruption . . ." (Galatians 6:7, 8).

Scripture associates overeating and alcohol abuse. In ancient Israel parents were to bring stubborn, rebellious, and disobedient children before the leaders of the city and say, for example, ". . . he is a glutton, and a drunkard. And all the men of his city shall stone him with stones, that he die . . ." (Deuteronomy 21:20, 21). Solomon said: "Be not among winebibbers; among riotous eaters of flesh: For the drunkard and the glutton shall come to poverty . . . (Proverbs 23:20, 21).

Paul spoke of the relationship between the flesh and the spirit: "they that are after the flesh do mind the things of the flesh. . . . For to be carnally minded is death . . . if ye live after the flesh, ye shall die . . ." (Romans 8:5, 6, 13). Many

Christians and pagans alike tragically embrace the philosophy: "Let us eat and drink; for to morrow we shall die" (Isaiah 22:13; *see also* 1 Corinthians 15:32). In the context of the holiness of our God-given bodies, Paul said: "Meats for the belly, and the belly for meats: but God shall destroy both it and them . . ." (1 Corinthians 6:13). Of the enemies of the cross, he wrote: "Whose end is destruction, whose God is their belly . . ." (Philippians 3:19).

Overeating is an addiction just as certainly self-destructive as drug abuse or alcoholism. For most people, especially men above thirty and women above forty-five years of age, underexercising can all too frequently contribute to premature heart attacks and death. Both sins result from habits and, with adequate motivation, can be changed.

Donna, a young mother of two, came to see me last year, referred by her family physician. "Dr. Andrews did a complete physical on me and found nothing wrong, except that I'm overweight. Otherwise I'm healthy, but I'm grossly unfit, he says, which would account for my problems. He told me you might be able to help me."

"Well," I answered, "as you know, I'm a psychiatrist. But I suspect he sent you to me because he knows I'm a Christian and a physical-fitness advocate. What do you think I can do to help you? What are your symptoms?"

"I don't think I need you as a psychiatrist," she responded. "Though if you can help me in that way, I'd be open to it. Except for my guilt about my constant craving for food and my obesity, I feel close to the Lord. Physically, though, I have some problems Dr. Andrews says you can help me with."

"What problems?"

"Well, first, I'm about fifty pounds overweight. I just never could seem to lose it after my last child was born. And now I've gained weight since then and just can't seem to get back down. My husband is beginning to complain. Only last week, he said that he still loved me as a person, but was beginning to be turned off by my 'ugly fat.' I guess it was that remark that got me to see Dr. Andrews." Her voice broke with a soft sob. I handed her a tissue, and she quickly composed herself.

"What specific physical changes have you become aware of, Donna?"

She looked up and wiped her eyes again. "Well, several: shortness of breath, walking upstairs or running to the telephone; feeling tired all day; sleepiness in the afternoon; difficulty picking up something on the floor or even getting my shoes on. Also I find I'm easily irritated by the kids and often have feelings of depression. I've lost interest in keeping the house clean, and I've begun missing the weekly mothers' Bible class at church. Dr. Hyder, I used to be one of the leaders of it!"

"Hmm—your weight problem is affecting every area of your life, isn't it? Any sexual problems?"

"Yes, I can't seem to reach a climax as easily as I used to. I never reject my husband, but he's beginning to complain that I'm too passive and unresponsive to his lovemaking."

"What do you think could account for all these problems, considering you've been checked out as being medically healthy?" I asked her.

"I'm so unfit and overweight, I guess," she replied.

"Okay," I said. "The cure lies entirely with you. Dr. Andrews and I can advise you, but you have to do the work. It depends on your own enthusiasm and motivation. If you desire to lose weight and get fit we can help, but you've got to want to do it."

"I'm motivated plenty now," Donna quickly responded. "I'm scared of losing my husband. I want to feel and function better—to get rid of my symptoms and regain my sense of self-respect."

"Good. Now here's the answer. It's as simple as two and two make four.

"Every pound of fat in your body is the equivalent of thirty-five hundred calories. You take in calories by eating or drinking anything but water. You lose them by exercise. Every time you take in thirty-five hundred calories more than you put out, you inevitably gain one pound in weight—all fat. The opposite is also true. Burn up thirty-five hundred calories more than you take in, and you'll lose a pound."

"Sounds pretty straightforward, but how do I actually *do* it?" she asked.

"A combination of diet and exercise. Eat less and exercise more. You need both, Donna. One without the other usually doesn't work."

"All right. What kind of diet and what kind of exercise?" she asked a little halfheartedly.

"The best diet is to eat what you know is both enjoyable and good for you nutritionally, but less than you're used to eating. Don't go on a special diet, just eat smaller portions of what you usually like. Leave the table, at the end of each meal, feeling still a little hungry. Ten minutes later your stomach will have fully stretched, and you won't feel hungry again until the next mealtime."

"No special diet?" she queried somewhat unbelievingly.

"Certainly no low-this or high-that kind of fad diet," I said. "They all make you lose weight too quickly, and nine out of ten dieters get so sick and tired of the deprivation that they give up and gain the weight back again. Be patient and satisfied with a weight loss of one pound per week. This way will not only be easier and less painful for you, but also your whole metabolic system will have time to adapt to the slightly lowered intake, and you won't have any reactive cravings to go on a binge."

"No restrictions then: just eat slightly less of everything. It sounds a lot less painful than some of the diets I've tried before," she said. "And you're right, every time I lost a few pounds, I put them right back on again."

"No real restrictions," I reassured her, "but be sensible about foods that you know are just empty calories with little food value. Be especially careful to cut down on anything containing sugar or animal fat, and don't forget that alcohol is turned into sugar by the liver, so watch that, too."

"I don't drink, so that's not a problem," she said. "But now what about vitamin supplements?"

"Good question," I replied, "because it's hard to answer. Some people who eat mainly supermarket-type, frozen, processed, or packaged food need some vitamin and mineral supplements. I suspect that most city and suburban dwellers need some nowadays, but if you could try to increase your intake of fresh fruits and vegetables and try to avoid mass-produced packaged foods, you probably don't need them. Most farmers or other country dwellers, for example, eat much fresher food than urban people and usually don't need supplements. But a daily type couldn't hurt you."

"Okay. Anything else about the diet?" she asked.

"Yes, try to reduce the frequency with which you eat pork, bacon, ham, beef, or lamb, because they are all so fatty. Try to develop a taste for chicken, turkey, veal or fish instead. They are just as nutritious, but far less fatty. Lower in calories, too!"

"I love fish," she said, "so that shouldn't be difficult, but I guess I've really got to resist cookies and ice cream."

"Yes, and also get into the habit of looking at the list of ingredients on anything you consider buying in a store. If sugar is one of the first three mentioned, you probably should leave it on the shelf."

"Oh—," she sighed. "You mentioned exercise. I can't do anything too vigorous. I just get too tired. What would you suggest?"

"Walking is the best. It's the easiest, most convenient, and least expensive, but it takes time. It burns up six calories a minute, or three-hundred-sixty calories an hour, if you walk at the fairly brisk pace of four miles per hour. If you could walk for one hour each day and reduce your intake by just one-hundred-forty calories, that would make a total of five hundred calories more burned up than those taken in. Five hundred times seven is thirty-five-hundred, which you remember is the number of calories in every pound of fat. At the end of one week you'll weigh one pound less. This time next year you will have lost all fifty pounds. That may seem far off, but just think about what you were doing this time last year, and it probably seems like yesterday! When you start seeing progress, the time will pass quickly."

"You're right. You make it sound so easy; there must be a catch in it somewhere!" she responded.

"It's really not difficult, if you have the motivation," I said. "Also you may have to vary it according to your other daily or weekly duties. For example, if you could only walk for half an hour one day, that would burn up one-hundred-eighty calories, and you'd have to reduce your intake by three-hundred-twenty calories to total the five hundred. On the other hand, if one day you found that you had the time to walk for an hour and a half, you'd burn up over five hundred calories, and you wouldn't need to deprive yourself of any intake at all, but still stay away from sugar and animal fat. Get yourself a calorie-counter book from the supermarket and learn the caloric values of what you eat.

"You've got to be patient. After all you've gained the

weight over a period of years. Don't try to lose it in a few weeks. You'll simply gain it back. Give yourself several months. It works far better."

Donna went off determined to be successful this time, saying she'd see me again in a month.

"I've lost five pounds since I last saw you," she beamed, when she returned. "Cutting out the sugar and fatty stuff was really hard at first, but I'm getting used to it now, I guess!

"I found an hour of brisk walking a bit tough the first week or so, so I started with just half an hour, but I can do an hour a day easily now. I can already tell I'm getting fitter as well as losing weight. I haven't felt so healthy in years! Is there anything else I can be doing?" she asked.

"Well, sounds as if you really have reason to be pleased with yourself," I encouraged. "Anything else, huh? Well, you can add plenty of variety to the program. As far as food

is concerned, if you eat plenty of green vegetables and still stay away from sugar and fat, you can look forward to three moderate-sized meals each day of virtually any food that appeals to you. With regard to the exercise, you can do lots of different aerobic activities."

"I've heard of aerobic dancing. Just what does *aerobic* mean, Dr. Hyder?" she asked eagerly.

"Essentially, an aerobic exercise or dance is one that involves increased exchange of air; it raises your rate of breathing, which automatically increases your heart rate," I replied. "It leads to total fitness, which is a combination of improved cardiorespiratory endurance, with increased muscular strength and flexibility.

"Walking is a good example. Your heart and lungs go faster when you are walking than when you are standing still, sitting, or lying down. Other aerobic sports are bicycling, swimming, skiing, skating, skipping rope, handball, various racquet sports, and probably best of all, jogging or running. Most team sports are also intermittently aerobic, but they are not relevant to your situation."

"Well, I've got a bicycle, and I like to swim," she said. "How would they compare with walking?"

"Bicycling at about ten miles per hour would be about the equivalent of walking at four miles per hour," I said. "Swimming, say an easy breaststroke, would be also approximately equivalent in terms of minutes and calories. However, the Australian crawl would be almost double the value, but you shouldn't attempt that at this stage for more than a few seconds."

"Why not?" she asked.

"You mustn't overdo it!" I said. "Be patient. Be content to lose one pound a week and eventually to achieve aerobic fitness. Stick with the program, and you'll feel ten years younger a year from now, I promise. Don't go to excess either with the diet or the exercise. Excess with the diet could lead to malnutrition; excess with any exercise could lead to muscle or joint injury or even a heart attack, in an extreme situation."

She came back a month later, having lost another five pounds. "I guess your program is working," she started. "I think I've really kicked the sugar habit, and I'm walking so fast now that I think I'm ready to run!"

"Fine," I responded. "Start off then at scout's pace. Do you know what that is?"

"My son mentioned it once," she said with a questioning look on her face.

"It's a method of crossing the countryside used by the Boy Scouts since the early part of this century," I told her. "Lord Baden-Powell, their founder, devised it during the Boer War as a means of covering the maximum distance on foot in a day. Simply jog fifty paces, then walk fifty paces; jog and walk alternately fifty paces at a time. You'll find you can cover a mile every twelve minutes. If you can keep it up for an hour, you'll have covered five miles and easily burned up your daily five hundred calories.

"As you continue to improve your aerobic fitness you may eventually want to jog continuously. You could probably comfortably run at a pace of ten minutes per mile. If you did, you'd burn up ten calories per minute, one hundred calories per mile, and six hundred in an hour. If you want to do this, though, I *do* advise that you buy yourself a pair of running shoes. Ordinary tennis sneakers could cause foot or ankle injuries."

Donna stuck with her program, and sure enough she lost her fifty pounds in a year. She has maintained a healthy weight ever since by continuing to control her sugar and fat intake and going for an hour's jog three or four times every week. She has even persuaded her husband to join her on weekends, which helps to keep *his* heart in good shape and provides time alone together, too. She feels and functions much better in all areas, and her marital and family relationships are now all very happy.

Bounding with joy across the miles.

Readers interested in following Donna's example in weight loss are urged to study the six appendixes at the end of the book. These will aid in establishing a program of weight loss through diet control and increased exercise.

Too many Christians have regarded their physical bodies as burdens, rather than gifts from God. In a letter to the Corinthians, Paul said: "What? know ye not that your body is the temple of the Holy Ghost which is in you, which ye have of God, and ye are not your own? For ye are bought with a price; therefore glorify God in your body, and in your spirit, which are God's" (1 Corinthians 6:19, 20). Finally he admonished the Romans: "I beseech you therefore, brethren, . . . that ye present your bodies a living sacrifice, holy, acceptable unto God, which is your reasonable service" (Romans 12:1).

Questions

1. Share your attitudes toward physical exercise. Do you enjoy it or avoid it? Tell why you enjoy it, if you do. Confess why you avoid it, if you do.

2. What is your personal belief in regard to the sin of gluttony? Are you tolerant of it in others, in yourself? What do you understand to be God's requirement of you in the matter of taking care of your physical body?

3. How do you react to the recommendations made to Donna about a gradually escalating exercise program? If you agree in principle, are you willing to follow them yourself and urge your friends and loved ones to do the same?

4. Discuss with others your understanding of caloric input and output as a measure of body weight as expounded by the figures in Appendix B. Can you share about other

forms of aerobic activity not mentioned here that could be equally valid for caloric balance?

5. Think, pray through, and discuss the scriptural passages in this chapter: Galatians 6:7, 8; Deuteronomy 21:20, 21; Proverbs 23:20, 21; Romans 8:5, 6, 13; Isaiah 22:13; 1 Corinthians 15:32; 1 Corinthians 6:13; Philippians 3:19; 1 Corinthians 6:19, 20; Romans 12:1.

For Further Study

Cooper, Kenneth H. *The Aerobics Way.* New York: M. Evans, 1977.

Fixx, James F. *The Complete Book of Running.* New York: Random House, 1977.

German, Donald R. *Too Young to Die.* New York: Farnsworth, 1974.

Glasser, William. *Positive Addiction.* New York, Harper & Row, 1976.

Higdon, Hal. *Fitness After Forty.* Mountain View, Calif.: Anderson World, 1974.

Hoyt, Creig et al. *Food for Fitness.* Mountain View, Calif.: World, 1974.

Hyder, O. Quentin. *Shape Up.* Old Tappan, N.J.: Fleming H. Revell, 1979.

Krafft, James. *Flab: The Answer Book.* Old Tappan, N.J.: Fleming H. Revell, 1983.

Lance, Kathryn. *Running for Health and Beauty: A Complete Guide for Women.* New York: Bobbs-Merrill, 1977.

Lovett, C. S. *Help Lord—The Devil Wants Me Fat!* Baldwin Park, Calif.: Personal Christianity, 1977.

Appendix A
Weight Charts

Desirable weights in pounds for adult men and women, according to height and frame, in light (summer) indoor clothing with pockets empty and no shoes.

Men Aged Twenty-five and Over

Height	Small Frame	Medium Frame	Large Frame
5 1	112–120	118–129	126–141
5 2	115–123	121–133	129–144
5 3	118–126	124–136	132–148
5 4	121–129	127–139	135–152
5 5	123–133	130–143	138–156
5 6	128–137	134–147	142–161
5 7	132–141	138–152	147–166
5 8	136–145	142–156	151–170
5 9	140–150	146–160	155–174
5 10	144–154	150–165	159–179
5 11	148–158	154–170	164–184
6 0	152–162	158–175	168–189
6 1	156–167	162–180	173–194
6 2	160–171	167–185	178–199
6 3	164–175	172–190	182–204

Young people between eighteen and twenty-five years, subtract one pound for each year under twenty-five. Consult pediatrician's charts for adolescents and children.

For nude weight, deduct three pounds for men and two pounds for women.

Women Aged Twenty-five and Over

Height	Small Frame	Medium Frame	Large Frame
4 8	92– 98	96–107	104–119
4 9	94–101	98–110	106–122
4 10	96–104	101–113	109–125
4 11	99–107	104–116	112–128
5 0	102–110	107–119	115–131
5 1	105–113	110–122	118–134
5 2	108–116	113–126	121–138
5 3	111–119	116–130	125–142
5 4	114–123	120–135	129–146
5 5	118–127	124–139	133–150
5 6	122–131	128–143	137–154
5 7	126–135	132–147	141–158
5 8	130–140	136–151	145–163
5 9	134–144	140–155	149–168
5 10	138–148	144–159	153–173

Weight charts used by courtesy of the Metropolitan Life Insurance Company.

Appendix B
Caloric Intake

A significant percentage of American adults over thirty years of age eat more food than they need to sustain a stable, healthy weight. The older one gets, the slower becomes one's Basal Metabolic Rate, and the easier it is to gain weight. Below is a chart of intake of calories needed daily to maintain desirable weight, based on moderate activity.

Those living a very sedentary life-style should subtract at least 300 calories; those leading a very physically active life may add 300 calories to these figures. Calories may also be added on the basis of aerobic exercise expenditure (*see* Appendixes C and D).

Remember: Food is calories in, is weight gain. Exercise is calories out, is weight loss. Daily maintenance calories are:

| | Women | | | | Men | | |
DESIRABLE WEIGHT	18–35 YEARS	35–55 YEARS	55–75 YEARS	DESIRABLE WEIGHT	18–35 YEARS	35–55 YEARS	55–75 YEARS
99	1,700	1,500	1,300	110	2,200	1,950	1,650
110	1,850	1,650	1,400	121	2,400	2,150	1,850
121	2,000	1,750	1,550	132	2,550	2,300	1,950
128	2,100	1,900	1,600	143	2,700	2,400	2,050
132	2,150	1,950	1,650	154	2,900	2,600	2,200
143	2,300	2,050	1,800	165	3,100	2,800	2,400
154	2,400	2,150	1,850	176	3,250	2,950	2,500
165	2,550	2,300	1,950	187	3,300	3,100	2,600

Prepared by the Food and Nutrition Board of the National Academy of Sciences, National Research Council.

Appendix C
Caloric Expenditures of Various Activities

These are the approximate number of calories expended per minute, per ten minutes, and per hour, for an average 170-pound man. Reduce by 20 percent for an average 130-pound woman. Also see Appendix D for a more detailed chart on expenditures in running, based on body weight and pace.

	CALORIC EXPENDITURE		
Activity	Per Minute	Per Ten Minutes	Per Hour
Sleeping	1	10	60
Sitting and talking	1.25	12.5	75
Standing	1.5	15	90
Strolling at less than two mph; light housework; gardening; raking leaves	2	20	120
Walking three mph; cycling six mph; bowling; cleaning windows, mopping floors, vacuuming; mowing grass; horseback riding	4	40	240
Table tennis; fencing; volleyball; tennis, squash, racquetball or badminton doubles; golf (carrying own clubs); calisthenics; ballet exercises; modern dance; scrubbing floors; shoveling snow	5	50	300
Walking four mph; cycling ten mph; ice or roller skating for fun; baseball; gymnastics	6	60	360
Walking five mph; cycling eleven mph; tennis, racquetball singles	7	70	420
Jogging five mph; cycling twelve mph; running in place; swimming breaststroke laps nonstop; badminton singles	8	80	480
Jogging six mph, cycling fourteen mph; basketball; squash or handball singles; downhill skiing; competitive ice or roller skating	11	110	660

Activity	CALORIC EXPENDITURE		
	Per Minute	Per Ten Minutes	Per Hour
Running seven mph; boxing or wrestling; swimming crawl stroke. (Seven mph is just over eight and a half minutes per mile, a good running pace for those past thirty-five.)	13	130	780
Running eight mph; skipping rope. (Eight mph is seven and a half minutes per mile, a good aim for those under thirty-five.)	15	150	900
Race rowing; cross-country skiing; running ten mph	19	190	1,140
Marathon winner (26.2 miles in two hours ten minutes or over twelve mph)	23	230	1,380

Appendix D
Caloric Cost of Running

CALORIES USED PER MINUTE OF RUNNING

Weight (In pounds)	Pace per Mile (In Minutes and Seconds)								
	5:20	6:00	6:40	7:20	8:00	8:40	9:20	10:00	10:40
120	15.6	13.8	12.1	10.9	9.9	9.0	8.3	7.6	7.0
130	16.9	14.8	13.2	11.8	10.7	9.7	8.9	8.2	7.6
140	18.1	15.9	14.1	12.6	11.5	10.5	9.6	8.8	8.1
150	19.4	17.0	15.1	13.5	12.3	11.2	10.2	9.4	8.7
160	20.6	18.1	16.1	14.5	13.0	11.8	10.9	10.0	9.3
170	21.9	19.2	17.0	15.3	13.8	12.7	11.5	10.6	9.8
180	23.1	20.2	18.0	16.2	14.6	13.3	12.2	11.2	10.4
190	24.4	21.3	19.0	17.0	15.4	14.0	12.9	11.8	10.9
200	25.6	22.4	19.9	17.9	16.2	14.8	13.5	12.4	11.5
210	26.9	23.6	20.9	18.7	17.0	15.5	14.1	13.0	12.1
220	28.1	24.7	21.9	19.6	17.8	16.2	14.8	13.6	12.6

CALORIES USED PER MILE OF RUNNING

Weight (In pounds)	Pace per Mile (In Minutes and Seconds)								
	5:20	6:00	6:40	7:20	8:00	8:40	9:20	10:00	10:40
120	83	83	81	80	79	78	77	76	75
130	90	89	88	87	85	84	83	82	81
140	97	95	94	93	92	91	89	88	87
150	103	102	101	99	98	97	95	94	93
160	110	109	107	106	104	103	101	100	99
170	117	115	113	112	111	109	107	106	105
180	123	121	120	119	117	115	114	112	111
190	130	128	127	125	123	121	120	118	117
200	137	135	133	131	129	128	126	124	123
210	143	141	139	137	136	134	132	130	129
220	150	148	146	144	142	140	138	136	135

Remember: Expenditure of every 3,500 calories in excess of body's caloric intake equals a weight loss of one pound.

Appendix E
Contraindications to
Strenuous Exercise

There are some, fortunately rare, medical conditions that would preclude strenuous exercise. You *must* ask your family physician about these if you have any known symptoms that you suspect might endanger you with much increased activity. These conditions include:

1. Acute or severe chronic disorders of the heart's condition, efficiency, or rhythm.
2. Blockage (thrombosis or embolism), narrowing (stenosis or sclerosis) or weakening (aneurysm) of major blood vessels.
3. High diastolic blood pressure (lower figure, heart at rest), above 105 mm Hg.
4. Need for fixed-rate pacemakers.
5. Taking medications affecting heart rate, such as digitalis.
6. Any angina (heart pain across the front of the chest).
7. Severe shortness of breath from any disease of the lungs.
8. Acute infections or fevers such as influenza or those of the upper or lower respiratory tract.
9. Anemia of any cause.
10. Any serious blood chemical imbalance.
11. Uncontrolled diabetes.
12. Toxic or hypoactive thyroid or other serious endocrine disorder.
13. Pregnancy at thirty-five to forty weeks. (A woman in the earlier weeks of uncomplicated pregnancy may exercise lightly.)
14. Toxemia during pregnancy.
15. Kidney disease such as nephritis.
16. Liver disease such as hepatitis.
17. Serious acute or chronic muscular, arthritic, or bone disorders.

18. Marked obesity (over fifty pounds above average for height and frame).
19. Certain other uncontrolled metabolic disorders.
20. Overt psychotic conditions with reality-contact loss.

Appendix F
Scriptural References

DATE DUE

7/19/89			
7/30/8			
12/9/93			
07/09/95			
12/15/96			

DEMCO 38-297